Praise for *Class with the Countess*:

"[The Countess] knows a few things about breeding and tact."
—*The New York Times*

"Want a crash course in manners from New York's favorite countess? You're in for a sexy ride.... [*Class with the Countess*] is prim, useful, and often humorous.... Go straight to her chapter on the art of seduction. It's something she knows plenty about."
—*Daily News* (New York)

"Being an extremely low-born and gauche person, I rely heavily on the Countess for tips on good manners and etiquette. She has also taught me how to be more sassy and alluring."
—Simon Doonan, author of *Eccentric Glamour*

"Forget what you think you know from television: this lady walks the walk and talks the talk. She's a real doll, comfortable in her own skin and real, and if you're thinking about buying this book, it's one you will keep for yourself and send to friends who—like you—didn't know they needed it."   —Whoopi Goldberg

"My collections are about giving opportunities to women to express their feminine side. LuAnn understands the importance of femininity and shares her savoir-faire with you in this book."
—Catherine Malandrino, fashion designer

© MARILI FORASTIERI

Countess LuAnn de Lesseps is one of the six stars of Bravo's hit reality show *The Real Housewives of New York City* and has taught etiquette on numerous morning television shows. She lives with her family in New York and the Hamptons. Her Web site is www.classwiththecountess.com.

Diane Reverand has spent her life in book publishing as an innovative editor, editor in chief, and publisher at Doubleday, Random House, and HarperCollins. Known for her ability to discover and develop major publishing franchises, she currently enjoys working on the other side of the desk as a coauthor. She lives in Connecticut with her husband.

CLASS WITH THE

Countess

How to Live with Elegance and Flair

COUNTESS LUANN DE LESSEPS
with
DIANE REVERAND
ILLUSTRATIONS BY NICOLE NADEAU

GOTHAM BOOKS

GOTHAM BOOKS
Published by Penguin Group (USA) Inc.
375 Hudson Street, New York, New York 10014, U.S.A.

Penguin Group (Canada), 90 Eglinton Avenue East, Suite 700, Toronto, Ontario M4P 2Y3, Canada (a division of Pearson Penguin Canada Inc.); Penguin Books Ltd, 80 Strand, London WC2R 0RL, England; Penguin Ireland, 25 St Stephen's Green, Dublin 2, Ireland (a division of Penguin Books Ltd); Penguin Group (Australia), 250 Camberwell Road, Camberwell, Victoria 3124, Australia (a division of Pearson Australia Group Pty Ltd); Penguin Books India Pvt Ltd, 11 Community Centre, Panchsheel Park, New Delhi–110 017, India; Penguin Group (NZ), 67 Apollo Drive, Rosedale, North Shore 0632, New Zealand (a division of Pearson New Zealand Ltd); Penguin Books (South Africa) (Pty) Ltd, 24 Sturdee Avenue, Rosebank, Johannesburg 2196, South Africa

Penguin Books Ltd, Registered Offices: 80 Strand, London WC2R 0RL, England

Published by Gotham Books, a member of Penguin Group (USA) Inc.

Previously published as a Gotham Books hardcover edition
First trade paperback printing, January 2010

1   3   5   7   9   10   8   6   4   2

Gotham Books and the skyscraper logo are trademarks of Penguin Group (USA) Inc.

Copyright © 2009 by Countess LuAnn de Lesseps
All rights reserved

The Library of Congress has catalogued the hardcover edition of this book as follows:
Lesseps, LuAnn de.
Class with the countess: how to live with elegance and flair / Countess LuAnn de Lesseps;
with Diane Reverand.
p.   cm
ISBN 978-1-592-40468-1 (hbk.)   978-1-592-40520-6 (pbk.)
1. Etiquette.   2. Charm.   3. Courtesy.   4. Conduct of life.   I. Reverand, Diane.   II. Title.
BJ1853.L47 2009
395—dc22   2008053250

Printed in the United States of America
Set in Adobe Garamond Pro, Grotesque MT, Golden Cockerel ITC, and Bickham Script
Designed by Sabrina Bowers

While the author has made every effort to provide accurate telephone numbers and Internet addresses at the time of publication, neither the publisher nor the author assumes any responsibility for errors, or for changes that occur after publication. Further, the publisher does not have any control over and does not assume any responsibility for author or third-party Web sites or their content.

*Penguin is committed to publishing works of quality and integrity.
In that spirit, we are proud to offer this book to our readers;
however, the story, the experiences, and the words
are the author's alone.*

THIS BOOK IS DEDICATED TO:

My husband, the count,
without whom there would be no countess;

My children,
who inspire and delight me;

Princess Hohenlohe,
for the book she never did get to write;

And my parents and my family,
who are responsible for the woman I am today.

Contents

$\mathscr{P}$ART ONE:
The Art of Being Yourself
(in Any Situation)

𝒫ART TWO:
The Art of Making
Other People Comfortable

PART THREE:
The Art of Seduction

Acknowledgments

I like to send notes of appreciation, and I'm making this one public. First, I would like to thank all of you who wrote to me with questions and asked me for my advice. This book would not have happened without your encouragement—you've been my absolute inspiration.

Being on *The Real Housewives of New York City* gave me the opportunity to share my life with the viewers whose response was so enthusiastic. I thank Lauren Zalaznick, Andy Cohen, and Christian Barcellos of Bravo for believing in the countess. And I would like to thank Ricochet Television and everyone involved in the production, especially Jenn O'Connell and Keira Brings. Of course, I can't forget my new extended family, Jill, Bethenny, Alex, Ramona, and Kelly.

I am deeply grateful to everyone who has helped me to write and publish *Class with the Countess*. My friends and family have been so supportive as I just about disappeared to write this book in such a short time for the new season of *The Real Housewives of*

New York City. I'd try out ideas with them, and they were indispensable when they read early drafts of the manuscript and gave me their comments—so thank you, Ann-Marie Porter, Michael and Paula Nadeau, Mae Mougin, Zilia Sicre, Barbara K, and Sally Terry. Your insights and contributions added a whole new dimension to the book.

David Vigliano, my literary agent, had faith in me from the start. He has great vision, and he knew that people wanted not only an etiquette book, but were also interested in my stories. He introduced me to Diane Reverand, a publishing legend, who helped me with the concept and the writing. Without her, this book would never have been finished. We spent many hours at my kitchen table, working on the manuscript with an occasional break for a chicken Caesar salad and ginger tea. Thanks also go to Mike Harriot of the Vigliano Agency and Paul Schindler, the best entertainment attorney in town.

Special thanks go to Marili Forastieri, who has such a good eye for style and has taken some of the best photos of me, including the cover of this book. Thanks so much to Terri Gold, a dear friend, who has always been there to take pictures of special occasions in our lives. And my niece Nicole Nadeau for doing such a great job with the illustrations.

And then there are all the wonderful people at Gotham Books: William Shinker, my extraordinary publisher; Lauren Marino, my brilliant editor; Brianne Ramagosa, her outstanding assistant; Sabrina Bowers from the design department; and Lindsay Gordon from publicity—all have given me great direction, they are consummate professionals, and I don't worry about a thing knowing they are in charge.

I've saved my family for last, though they are always at the top of my list. My mother, brothers, and sisters helped me to remember how we were as we grew up. Alex read the manuscript with a published author's eye and was such a help in remembering the highlights of our life together. My children, who were so forgiving of my preoccupation with the book but were also my toughest critics. Thanks for your patience and understanding.

With **Real Housewives** *costar Jill Zarin*

(PHOTO BY ROB RICH)

INTRODUCTION

How Does a Countess Come to Be on Reality TV?

Since the first season of *The Real Housewives of New York City* began to air, I have been deluged with e-mails and letters asking my advice on everything from what to wear to knowing what to say, from table manners to how to radiate self-confidence. Little did I expect the response my appearance on the show would generate. It became obvious that people are confused about what is appropriate in a world in which anything goes, and fans were turning to me for advice. People seem just as eager to know my story, especially how I became a countess, and are curious about what being an aristocrat means today. I decided to address all of the many questions I have received by combining my story, the life lessons I have learned along the way, and my distinctive advice on how to navigate our sometimes rude world with elegance, by writing *Class with the Countess*.

Naturally, one of the first questions people ask is why I agreed to take a role in the show.

Though you might not expect a countess to participate in a reality show, the decision to appear on *Real Housewives of New York City* came easily to me. I have always been daring and adventurous, as you will soon see.

When I received an e-mail from my friend Jill Zarin, offering to talk to me about appearing on a show to be called *Manhattan Moms*, I was definitely curious. But let me start at the beginning.

I met Jill Zarin at the after-party of a screening of Michael Moore's movie *Sicko* that I had attended with my niece Coryn. At one point, I looked over to see my niece talking with an older gentleman. I joined them and learned that Bobby Zarin had invited Coryn to the Zarins' Fourth of July party so that his son could meet her. We had a lively conversation, and Jill Zarin joined us. We really hit it off, and our paths continued to cross. That's how it is in New York—it can feel like a small town sometimes.

My family went off to Europe for a few weeks. While our children attended camp in Switzerland, my husband and I vacationed with our friends Sebastian and Elizabeth in the South of France. The day we returned, I found the e-mail from Jill about the show. I took the leap and met with the producers.

I decided to do the show for a number of reasons. First, I wanted the history of the de Lesseps family to be better known in the United States. They are so respected in Europe and little known here. From building the Suez Canal to presenting the Statue of Liberty to the United States for the French, their international contributions have been exemplary and deserve more recognition in my own country.

In addition, I wanted people to know that a countess does more than shop, have lunch with her girlfriends, and get her nails done. I hoped to draw attention to the charities with which my husband and I are involved. After all, Alex received The Fulbright Humanitarian Award in 2005 for his work in creating Myanmar Children's Association and in microfinance, bridging the gap between rich and poor.

I also thought it would be fun for our children, Victoria and Noel, to experience the TV world. Not only would they develop poise and learn how to handle themselves in any situation, but they would also get an education on how a TV show is produced, the lighting, the various technicians, and all the work that goes into making an hour of TV a week.

Finally, I viewed the opportunity as a challenge. I had been a TV personality in Europe and on the morning TV circuit here, but I had never done reality TV. I am always one to rise to a challenge, to take risks, and to try new things. This impulse has expanded my world and made me a more rounded person. Being part of *The Real Housewives of New York City* has been everything I expected and more, and the correspondence I have received inspired me to write this book.

What I've learned is that people are dying to bring civility back. They are tired of being treated badly, and they are tired of seeing people behave badly. We have a take-out culture, and social graces have been tossed out with the plastic containers. We are constantly assaulted by offensive, coarse, selfish behavior. I have a number of pet peeves: being treated to others' cell phone conversations in elevators, the enthusiastic chewing of gum in public, people who talk too

> We have a take-out culture, and social graces have been tossed out with the plastic containers.

much—especially about money—and don't know how to listen and ask questions, the sight of jeans and running shoes at the theater or opera, the vision of a maniac walking down the street while talking loudly and gesticulating wildly during a Bluetooth conversation. I could go on. No doubt you could add many more annoyances to my quick list.

I sense a growing desire for something better—for manners, refinement, and consideration. So many people have asked me to write a book on etiquette. They want to reduce their social anxiety by learning the rules. But being gracious involves so much more than that. Consider how the meaning of etiquette evolved.

> I sense a growing desire for something better—for manners, refinement, and consideration.

Etiquette was originally a Keep Off the Grass sign. King Louis XIV's gardeners at Versailles could not prevent the aristocrats invited to the king's lavish parties from ruining the lawns and gardens. They stuck signs—*etiquets*—into the ground, warning the partiers to "keep off the grass and don't walk on the flowers." Of course, the signs were ignored. The king finally had to decree that no one could go beyond the bounds of the signs. Later, an invitation to court functions was called *etiquette* (a ticket!), which indicated where to stand and what to do. Etiquette came to mean lists of ceremonial observances at court. Then the term broadened to mean the signs that tell us what to do in new situations. Today, etiquette has come to mean polite behavior in society.

Being a magnetic person requires more than knowing "not to go there," though that's certainly part of it. That's why this book is divided into three parts. In Part One, The Art of Being Yourself (in Any Situation), I show you that dealing with yourself comes first. To develop your charisma, you have to learn confidence—or at least how to fake it—as well as the most dazzling way to present yourself to the world. The next part, The Art of Making Other People Comfortable, involves dealing with others and considering their needs, or, in other words, learning social graces. From the art of conversation to everyday etiquette, from being a stellar hostess to being a perfect guest, from creating a gracious home to instilling manners in children,

> I believe all of life is a seduction.

this section focuses on the rules for becoming a social success. I have called Part Three The Art of Seduction, because I believe all of life is a seduction. Life is unquestionably richer if you can get everyone into your corner—from waiters to the service people in stores to the men in your life. Winning people over adds spice to life. It makes every encounter special.

In this book, I share with you how I learned to handle anything that comes my way with panache, and tips on how to be a gracious and charming person. How I came from humble roots as one of seven children living in a small town in Connecticut to my current life in New York, Gstaad, and the Hamptons as a countess, with many stops in European capitals and chic spots in the company of notable people along the way, is an entertaining and, I hope, inspiring story, full of crazy coincidences and a lot of luck. By telling my stories, I want to pass on what I've learned about finding the good in any situation and how to be comfortable anywhere, anyplace, anytime.

The greatest learning experience for me was the leap I made moving to Italy from New York. I arrived in Milan to model.

How I got there from working as a nurse in Connecticut involves my penchant for being daring and open to new possibilities. People are so afraid to take chances, but without taking risks and challenging yourself, how can you grow? You can always go home. I've learned everything I know by getting out there and doing it—with a little help from my friends. I've had wonderful mentors who helped to shape the person I am and how I live my life. I found my very generous mentors in Europe, where society runs on a different frequency from ours.

I fell in love with Italy and the Italian people. Everyone dressed so impeccably and had so much style. There was such elegance, sex appeal, and intensity in everyday life. People entertained, ate fabulous food, and drank great wine and strong espresso. They talked, talked, talked about everything passionately. People were not afraid to be friendly. They were open and warmhearted, so civilized with one another. Everyone had a natural level of courtesy. Men would open doors, get up when I entered a room, and look at me with bold admiration. Even young boys knew how to appreciate a woman. Everything about Italy appealed to my senses and my spirit. I came into my own in Italy and will tell you all about it.

I hope that imparting the experiences and lessons I have learned will help you to live a richer, more satisfying life—one animated by a profound joie de vivre.

COUNTESS LUANN DE LESSEPS

PART ONE

The Art of Being Yourself
(in Any Situation)

At home with my dog, Aston
(PHOTO BY MARILI FORASTIERI)

Being myself in Capri

(COURTESY OF THE AUTHOR)

What's Inside

ℱITTING IN ANYWHERE

Knowing all the rules of etiquette that exist will not guarantee that you will be a gracious and memorable person. That's why we will begin by considering the art of being yourself, which, in the end, is what "class" is all about. You don't have to be rich, famous, or noble to have an unforgettable presence. Money can't buy it, but you can certainly learn to be gracious and relaxed wherever you find yourself.

My father, Roland Nadeau, and my husband, Alexandre Count de Lesseps, have more elegance and charisma than anyone I have ever met. Their lives and backgrounds could not have been more different, yet they both have that remarkable quality known as class.

> You don't have to be rich, famous, or noble to have an unforgettable presence.

My father's mother was a full-blooded Native American of the Micmac tribe of the Algonquin Indians. He grew up poor in Canada, one of twelve children. My husband, Alex, is descended from an illustrious French family that traces its roots back to the fourteenth century. From the middle of the eighteenth century, the de Lesseps followed diplomatic careers. Napoleon I ennobled my husband's great-great-great-grandfather, Mathieu de Lesseps, giving him the title of count. His son, Ferdinand de Lesseps, also a diplomat, was awarded the commission to achieve his lifelong dream of building the Suez Canal. Napoleon III wanted to give him the title of Duke of Suez, but he declined because he wanted to keep his family title. In 1886, Ferdinand de Lesseps formally presented the Statue of Liberty to the United States for France.

Since his family served France as diplomats, Alex lived all over the world as he was growing up. He became adept at adjusting to new situations early on. Alex, a philanthropist, supports charities in every corner of the planet. My dashing husband was skiing on the slopes of Gstaad, where we happened to meet at a swanky dinner party (a story for later).

Alex has real savoir faire. He always knows the right thing to do, but he is the sort of man who rises above convention, who has the confidence and style to make his own rules. After all, he broke with tradition to marry me, an American girl from Connecticut who had become a television star in Italy.

Even though my father was not "to the manor born," he had great presence and awareness. He had a natural dignity and curiosity that allowed him to fit in anywhere. My father inspired me to be the person I am. He gave me the confidence to take chances and to be open to possibilities that presented themselves to me. And that willingness to try new things led me on an unexpected path to the love of my life.

CONFIDENCE IS THE KEY

As far as I'm concerned, "class" is an attitude. It's all about confidence. It's evident in the way you treat other people. If you are self-assured, comfortable with who you are, and respectful of other people, you can stop thinking about yourself and respond openly to others. I have to confess: I was born confident. Being a shrinking violet was never my style. But don't worry: If you don't possess a natural confidence, there are ways to gain confidence—or to fake it until you make it. Just being familiar with the etiquette guidelines I cover in Part Two will give you a boost.

QUICK CONFIDENCE BOOSTERS

- Remember: No one is perfect.
- Be thankful for what you have.
- Don't take yourself too seriously.
- Remind yourself that people are too concerned with their own shortcomings to notice yours.
- Set achievable goals.
- Be prepared—the Boy Scouts are right.
- Learn to silence your negative self-talk—pump yourself up with positive thinking.
- Rely on the advice of a mentor. If you don't have one, find one.
- Help others.
- Get active—the more you move, the more you get done.
- Smile—it really does affect how you feel.

I grew up with four older brothers and two sisters, one younger and the other older. I realize that growing up in such a large family taught me how to be considerate of others' needs by necessity, and how to stroke my siblings and my parents to get what I wanted. Having a big, genial family proved to be great experience for later in life. Since I had so many terrific brothers who were much older than I, I became accustomed to spending time with older kids, which boosted my self-confidence and helped me later when I encountered people who were more worldly than I was at the time. I also developed a

> Being comfortable in your own skin is a prerequisite for moving through life with ease.

healthy appreciation of men that has never left me. I am definitely a woman who loves men and appreciates the value of women.

To be a gracious and charming person, you have to be able get outside yourself, to overcome your own self-consciousness. Being comfortable in your own skin is a prerequisite for moving through life with ease. Being open to anything or anyone that comes your way is an attitude that will help you expand your horizons. My curiosity and risk-taking certainly made my life what it is today.

CHOOSING LA DOLCE VITA

I found my way to Milan and established myself in Italy with daring, perseverance, and buckets of luck. I had left my job as a nurse in Connecticut and was modeling in New York, but I needed to moonlight as a nurse to support myself. I would take a subway to

Queens, and the rest homes there were a far cry from those in Connecticut.

I went to Europe for the first time with a boyfriend—from Berlin, Connecticut, to the Berlin Wall. I had already decided to try my luck in Milan. Wide-eyed as we traveled everywhere, I couldn't believe this whole world existed. I was in discovery mode, and I couldn't get enough of it. At the time, I had no doubt that I was meant to stay in Europe.

When we reached Milan, my boyfriend didn't want to leave me behind in the little pensione I was staying in, but it was time for the long kiss good-bye. I didn't know a soul in Italy. I really didn't fit in. Everyone was so elegant and spoke at least three languages. I was alone and spoke no Italian at all. I did have a less than top modeling agency and a single phone number. Luckily, a friend in New York had given me the number of an aristocrat who lived with his mom—not uncommon, I would come to find out. I didn't think this fellow would bother to call me back. Genaldo del Bono did return my call, we became close friends, and eventually he was my lover.

Genaldo was like a Roman god—curly, dirty-blond hair, strong features, about my height—and he was worldly and charming. He introduced me to the most amazing people. It all seemed so sophisticated to me. I fell in love with the Italian life.

He knew everyone and was trying to help me. Genaldo believed in me and wanted me to be a success. He put me in touch with the big modeling agencies, but it was obvious that modeling wasn't going to work for me in Milan. I was too girl-next-door, I wasn't super-thin, and I didn't have a book of fashion work. There wasn't a lot of commercial modeling in Milan—it was all fashion, and I wasn't a fashion model. I ran out of money and had to return to New York.

Having experienced the cosmopolitan charm of the Europeans, I was frustrated and wanted to get back. Besides, I was crazy about Genaldo. He encouraged me to come back to participate in a beauty pageant for the Lady Universe title to be held in Cortina d'Ampezzo. I decided to take the leap. I wasn't about to let Europe beat me.

Forty girls were competing in the pageant—Miss Brazil, Miss France, Miss Yugoslavia—and I won. The prizes were a jeep and a necklace from God knows where, which I still have, tucked away with my sash. I had to make appearances all over Italy as Lady Universe. I was no longer just LuAnn, I was Lady *Universo*! Believe it or not, this is what opened up the door for me

My first title: "Lady Universo"
(COURTESY OF THE AUTHOR)

in Europe, because the moment you have a title, any title, you are in.

As Lady Universe, I met the *crème de la crème* and had to make appearances all over Europe. I visited Asti and met Dottore Roberto Gancia—you'll notice he has an honorary title of respect—who owned an Italian wine dynasty that produced Asti Spumante, among other fine wines. He was one of those men who get more handsome as they age. Sandy-haired with striking blue eyes, he was distinguished and aristocratic in bearing. To my surprise, he seemed interested in me.

I was still dating Genaldo, who took me to a party in Cortina in the Italian Alps, hosted by Prince Egon von Fürstenberg, the first husband of fashion icon Diane von Fürstenberg. Egon asked me what I was doing in Milan. When I told him about modeling, he suggested that I would have more success in television, because, he said, "Italians love Americans." He wasted no time following through.

That very evening, Egon introduced me to Johnny Manginelli, a producer at the Italian TV station Rai Uno. With great generosity, Egon asked him if he had anything for me in TV. Johnny Manginelli said, "Sì." He was casting a show the very next week in Rome. I took his card and followed up.

The producers hired me to do the show! I was to work with the leading TV show host, Milly Carlucci, who was a combination of Gina Lollobrigida and Kelly Ripa. Since I didn't speak Italian at that point, the only thing I could do was turn letters. I guess I was the Italian version of Vanna White.

Milly Carlucci had a manager named Ludovico Socci, who saw great promise in me and recommended that I learn Italian quickly. He thought if I could speak Italian, I would become a star. I signed up at the Berlitz school for an intensive Italian course and practiced on taxi drivers and everyone else I encountered. I landed a role on *Paperissima,* a show like *America's Funniest Home Videos.* Of course, I was one of the girls behind the star, turning letters once again.

I loved working in Italian TV—I could get contracts for six months or a year, rather than pounding the pavement as a model. I had hair and makeup every day and got to dress up.

Who wouldn't love that?

The Italians adopted me as their own. Everybody just loved the American girl. They loved showing me the ropes and expressed their enthusiasm openly. They were introducing me to everything and everybody. I'd get my derrière pinched on the bus. Boys would follow me home with love notes in their hands. There wasn't a day that I wasn't offered a café. This was nothing like New York, where a pretty woman could go unnoticed. The Italians made me feel like a woman, because they put me on a pedestal. I was living *la dolce vita,* the sweet life. New York was far from my mind.

Soon after we met, Roberto Gancia invited me to a party at his palatial estate. I wanted to look spectacular for the occasion. I was so self-conscious about my lack of experience and my age—only twenty-three years old at the time. Dressed in a slinky black floor-length gown, I stood out all right. All the other women were so chic in their simple cocktail dresses, little evening suits, and great jewelry. They were certainly not welcoming to the new girl in town. I felt out of place.

Of course, Dottore Gancia behaved with consummate grace. He took me by the arm and introduced me to his guests as a glamorous newcomer from the States whom they would soon be seeing a lot of on TV. Everyone was very generous to me. They even shifted from Italian to English whenever necessary to accommodate my rudimentary Italian.

Roberto Gancia saw a quality in me that he knew would evolve with his help. Over time, he replaced Genaldo in my affections. Roberto had a higher level of sophistication. I saw a quality in him I admired. And he didn't live with his mother. Much of my early education in the social graces came from Mr. Gancia, who opened my eyes to the intricate dance that took place at such high levels of society. Most importantly, he taught me about self-possession, mystery, dazzling presentation, how to carry myself, and how to dodge jealous Italian women. I certainly needed his advice. He continued to pursue me, eventually pushing Genaldo out of the scene.

He refined my taste in clothes, particularly shoes, which were top on his list. If I went shopping alone, he actually arranged for one of his staff to accompany me to carry my bags—a little strange for an American girl to be moving around Milan with a shadow shopper. Very bizarre! I had to convince him I could manage on my own.

*B*E CURIOUS AND LEARN FROM EVERYTHING AND EVERYONE

Early in my teens, I worked in a rest home owned by a family for whom I babysat. There I would be, talking with Mary, Dick, and Rose in their wheelchairs. Though my first job was to wash dishes, I loved spending time with them and hearing their stories, probably because I never knew my own grandparents. I have always suspected that my profound respect for older people derives from my Native American roots. Elders are so important in Native American culture. My experience of caring for the elderly as a teenager was what eventually led me to become a nurse.

I was curious and soaked up all I could from what the old folks said, and listened to their stories eagerly. And they appreciated my attention in return. I was particularly fond of one woman called Beatrice, who loved to talk about girl stuff—dating and boys. She lived vicariously through me and had the curiosity of a teenager at the age of eighty-six. I spent hours with her as I would a girlfriend of my own age. And she shared with me her wisdom and insight.

Being interested is what makes you interesting. The best defense against a lack of confidence is curiosity. Look outside yourself and everyday concerns to elevate your sensibilities, increase your sense of wonder, and intensify the pleasure you find in both familiar and uncommon events. Appreciate the best that life has to offer

> Being interested is what makes you interesting.

through work and travel. Take a cooking class or play golf, chess, or bridge. Learn to sail or ski. Join a gym. Take ballroom dancing or singing lessons. See all the independent movies, design and care for gorgeous gardens, collect classic jazz or learn a language.

BE DARING AND READY FOR ANYTHING

A stint working as the secretary to a bank president convinced me that office work was not for me. I went back to working in the rest home, became a practical nurse, and worked in Connecticut for three years. The work was much more rewarding to me.

One fateful day, a nurse's aide told me she wanted to be in the Miss Connecticut pageant. She encouraged me to do it with her. She even threatened that she wouldn't do it without me. I liked my job, but I was curious. I wasn't exactly beauty queen material. I was chubby, and my hair was big. And I had never been exposed to the insider tricks that gave the contestants a competitive edge. But that didn't stop me.

Nurse LuAnn
(COURTESY OF THE AUTHOR)

The decision to take a chance and to risk humiliating myself ended up changing my life.

No, I didn't win the pageant, but an official took a liking to me. "What do you do?" he asked me. "You should be modeling. You could make a lot of money."

And that's how life happens—being at the right place at the right time. The generous stranger told me about a modeling beauty competition in Hartford. He was sure I would win. Once again, I said, "Why not?" Each new experience is a step on the staircase of life.

Much to my surprise, I won. The first prize was a $500 photo shoot in New York City and representation by Mystique Model Management with offices in Hartford and New York. I took the bus to New York and had my picture taken. I resembled Jaclyn Smith in one shot. It worked! I started getting bookings from my card, and my life took an exciting turn to New York.

The motivating principle in my life is to take chances without fear or hesitation. Jump on the train or you'll miss it. I live that way. I've taken chances and followed my instincts. Nothing exciting would have happened to me if I had been timid and afraid. I'd probably still be living in Connecticut. And you know what? I'd still be happy, because I choose to be. You never miss what you never had.

A WORD ON PLEASURABLE PASTIMES

Who is more attractive than a person with interests and enthusiasms? Tennis is one of my favorites, because I love the social aspect of the sport. I play with my girlfriends, my husband, and sometimes even compete in tournaments. It's a great way to get exercise. I also love to sing—Bette Midler comes to mind—all kinds of music from cabaret to country rock.

Hobbies not only add passion to our lives, but they also add depth to our character.

Find something that interests you and go for it. It will give you energy and purpose. And don't be afraid to change it up now and then.

---

*C*HANGE FEELS BETTER THAN HABIT

Now, you might be at a point in your life that does not seem to afford you much choice, but you don't have to make a life-changing move to take a risk. I'm talking about not being afraid to change. Just switch up your routine a bit. Being rigid about anything will show on your face and in your body language and will limit you. The minute you think you are ripe, you begin to rot. You'll be surprised at the options available to you when you put a new foot forward.

> **The minute you think you're ripe, you begin to rot.**

Travel is a great way to expand your narrow, workday focus. If you are working hard to advance your career or run your household, you will want to make certain that you save money and make the time to explore. You don't have to travel to exotic places or spend a fortune to have the same effect.

Some of my best childhood memories are of road trips my family took together. All nine of us would pile into our station wagon with our luggage on the roof and hit the road. We had so much fun on the trip, it almost didn't matter where we were going. Some of my best trips have been just a train ride away. When I lived in Milan, I just hopped a train to travel to Venice, Florence, and Rome.

Being daring means you are ready to try something new and eager for fresh experiences and ideas. I find friends are great for that. Sally, an old friend, and I did the Princess Race, a rally for Innocence in Danger to raise money to send abused children to summer camp. It was a sport rally with events in kayaking, Jet Skiing, surfing, and skydiving. I had always wanted to skydive, but . . . Sally convinced me that if I didn't do it now, I would never do it. I succumbed to now-or-never peer pressure.

Rather than sign a release, we had to be videotaped saying we realized we could lose our lives participating in the event and that the Princess Race would not be liable for our deaths or any injuries sustained. If it hadn't been for the tall, dark, handsome Brazilian instructor, I would have walked home.

We proceeded to board a very small, ramshackle plane with a pilot who had many teeth missing. I was scared to death. Not only did I have to jump first since Sally weighed less than I (the bitch), but the pilot thought it was fun to use the "look-mom-no-hands" trick on me.

Stepping out of the door of the plane was like stepping onto the ledge of a building when you're about to jump. Oh my God! I knew then what they mean when they say, "You're not living if you don't have fear."

> If you don't think you're hot, nobody else will.

What they forgot to tell me before the event was not to wear shorts, because the harness holding you gives the worst wedgie. Don't bother to wear makeup either. As you fall, your face is like a tide pool—the ripple effect. I recommend jumping with a good-looking Brazilian. At least if you're going to die, it's with a hot guy.

MY CUP IS ALWAYS HALF FULL

Looking on the bright side is one of the most powerful ways to enhance your life. When I started to model, I shared my first apartment in New York City with two roommates. One worked on Wall Street and the other was in real estate. They would say to me, "There are hundreds of models trying to make it in New

York," "Don't get your hopes up," "We don't want you to get hurt," and other words of encouragement.

If you don't think you're hot, nobody else will was my motto. My early modeling days were strictly learn-as-you-go. I jumped into that world with a complete absence of savvy. I kept going to casting calls and was certain each time that I would get the job. If I didn't, I'd just move on to the next with the same conviction. Half the time, I would get the job because I was a nurse. Even though thousands of girls showed up for casting, I was chosen to shoot an ad campaign in Vale. Think about it from the client's point of view. Would you rather have a model/waitress on the slopes or a model/nurse?

Let's face it: Life is inevitably filled with ups and downs. Believing that things are bound to work out and that bad times will eventually pass can keep you on an even keel when life is less than perfect. To be a charismatic person, you can't be thrown completely off balance—or under the bus—by what life sends your way. You can rise above petty problems as well as serious adversity. Though we all have our sad, embarrassing, or anxious moments, we do have the power to choose how we view things.

One potentially mortifying experience comes to mind. I was with my dear friend and mentor Princess Hohenlohe (I'll tell you more about her later), the designer John Galliano, and Faycal Amor, the Moroccan designer and founder of Plein Sud, a very popular line of clothing in Europe during the eighties. We were heading out for an evening on the town in London. I was wearing a fabulous pair of high-heeled boots that I had borrowed from Faycal Amor after his runway show. As I walked down the palatial marble staircase to the lobby of the Barclay Hotel to meet my friends, both heels of the borrowed boots broke simultaneously, my legs flew out from under me, and I bumped down the gracefully curved staircase on my back, to the horror of everyone in the busy lobby. I slid across the marble floor with my legs practically over my head and came to a halt when I hit a splendid Persian carpet.

My friends were aghast, and even the hotel staff was frozen. I thought of the grand entrance I had hoped to make—and there I was sprawled in a most unflattering position in the lobby of one of the finest hotels in the world. When I saw the shocked expressions on the faces of guests and staff, I started to giggle, then broke into a full-throated laugh. The relief of everyone around me was palpable as John and Faycal helped me to my wobbly feet. This is where a sense of humor is always appealing. After I made a quick change, we laughed our way to dinner.

I could have rolled up in a ball and pretended I wasn't there, I could have cried with embarrassment, I could have feigned injury and had people fuss over me before retreating to my room, but I chose to view my carnival ride down the stairs as a slapstick moment. Fortunately, only my derrière and pride suffered slight bruising. I certainly wasn't about to let it ruin my evening.

Seeing the positive in any situation is an important part of elegance and charm. I am not suggesting that you become a Pollyanna—sophistication does require a firm grounding in reality, and there will certainly be problems and disappointment in life—but if you can see the best in yourself and the world around you, your life will be happier. You can be confident that you can handle—and even enjoy—whatever comes your way. If you are generous in your judgments of others, considering those you meet to be fascinating, trustworthy, and sensitive, your friendships and social encounters will be lively and rich. Your upbeat attitude will draw people to you, because being with you will make them feel good.

ℱAKE IT UNTIL YOU MAKE IT

When I made the decision to stay in Milan during my first trip to Europe, I was woefully unsophisticated, but I liked what I saw. I had absorbed a good deal from the modeling scene in New York, but in Italy I found myself at the Ivy League of style. Lucky for me, the Italians recognized that a little polish would really shine me up. I did meet a number of people who guided my education in the finer things of life, but for a time, I had to go it alone.

I observed with complete admiration the way the Italians lived. I would sit in cafés alone watching people pass on the street. What they wore, how they moved, their hand gestures, their animation, how they greeted each other, smoked their cigarettes, sipped their espresso, ate their pasta—nothing escaped me. I would walk through the streets in between "go-sees" and absorb the Italian life. I spoke minimal Italian but loved to listen to the rhythm of that beautiful language. I found myself understanding more and more. I have a musical ear—it felt like a song to me.

In retrospect, that brief period was one of the most thrilling times of my life. I was totally alone and doing anything was a challenge because of my limited funds and next to nonexistent Italian. I tried to fit in. I became a chameleon to behave like them. An instinctive ability to observe closely is another quality that I attribute

> We are shaped by the people we admire.

to my Native American heritage. I have always been able to notice the fine details and to mimic what I see. That's how I learned to model. I was self-taught. I would watch the girls walk and pose and would tell myself, "I can do that!"

The fact is that even if you have not yet discovered the best way to express your individuality and style or are not certain how to behave in different situations, you can look around and take your cue from others. If you are at a formal dinner, keep an eye on your hostess and follow her lead. If you are at other social events, just look around and observe what other guests are doing and how they dress. One of the helpful characteristics of elegance is that it is unmistakable. Finding role models should not be difficult, because memorable people worth emulating always stand out. You should focus on those who appeal to you, who epitomize everything you want to be. Whether it is a photo in a magazine, a scene in a movie or book, a woman walking down the street, or someone across a crowded room, you can identify with that person's look, tone, or way of behaving and add it to your repertoire. We are shaped by the people we admire.

> # Memorable people worth emulating always stand out.

GIVE AS MUCH AS YOU CAN

I am closing this chapter about the inner qualities that make you a fascinating person by discussing two subjects of great importance to me—social consciousness and charity. I am constantly aware of the abundance in my life, especially since I come from a humble background. I have worked hard since the age of fourteen as a babysitter, dishwasher, secretary, nurse's aide, practical nurse, aerobics instructor, model, and TV personality. I know how hard it is to make a living, and I recognize how much determination and sheer luck are necessary to get ahead. Then I think of people in third-world countries who have nothing, not even food or medicine for their children. We are so privileged, it's difficult for most of us to imagine a life without hope.

My charities are more to me than just gala social events. You might have seen me on the show helping a former drug addict prepare for a job interview for SoHo and TriBeCa Partnerships/ACE Program for the Homeless. I donate my time and experience as well as financial support. Since losing my father to cancer, I have become involved in fund-raising for the American Cancer Society. My husband and I have helped The Auditory/Oral School of Brooklyn for children with hearing problems, a charity with a special meaning for us since my husband lost the hearing in his left ear more than five years ago. Alex and I also have a fresh drinking water well charity and we help with the orphans of Myanmar. He has established Children of Myanmar Association, which builds schools and orphanages for girls and boys in that country. We also try to raise awareness by involving as many friends as possible.

You may not be able to donate a substantial amount of money to charity, but remember that there are always people who are a lot worse off than you and any contribution you can make will help. Look around you right at home to see who could use your help. Your neighbor may have lost his job. A friend may just have been diagnosed with cancer. A cousin may have lost his home. Whether it's making a meal, babysitting, or donating some clothes, think of things you can do personally to help.

And, of course, you can work for charities that need your help. You can volunteer to deliver meals to the elderly confined to their homes, be a teacher's aide in a school program that enlists the help of nonprofessionals, spend time with injured vets or help their families, serve a holiday meal at a soup kitchen, read to hospitalized children, or donate your services for a local charity auction if you have a business or a special skill. I've been giving time most recently to the Boys & Girls Club of Brooklyn mentoring teenagers. Since I do have a teenage daughter myself, I'm used to giving advice.

Compassion is a quality that takes you out of yourself and puts your troubles in perspective. We become so involved in our own problems and crises that it's easy to lose sight of the big picture. Remember: No matter where you find yourself on the misery scale, there is always someone who is much worse off than you. That realization should motivate you to help others. In doing so, you will reduce your own pain. I am reminded of a wake-up call in my own life.

While staying at a wonderful hotel in Florida with my family, I went to the spa to spend time in the sauna after a tennis match. I took off my beautiful and cherished wedding ring to wash my hands and put it on the shelf above the sink. I had a relaxing time in the sauna, took a quick shower, and returned to my room.

At dinner that night, I looked down at my hands and realized my diamond ring was missing. I didn't want to alarm Alex and hoped I would get my ring back. I made it through dinner and ran to the spa. The ring was nowhere to be found, and no one had turned it in. After I grilled the hotel staff, I realized it was gone.

I was heartbroken, and I was also worried that Alex would be really angry with me. I had lost our wedding ring! It was a valuable diamond, yet its meaning was even more important to me. Just as I was getting ready to tell him—you can imagine how I dreaded it—I received a call from a friend who lived in Florida near to where we were staying.

My friend was distraught. While in the care of a nanny, her precious grandson had wandered out to the pool while his mother was out to lunch. You know the rest of this terrible story.

In light of the nightmare my friend was going through and the pain she would feel for the rest of her life, how could I possibly be so concerned about a piece of jewelry? My problem seemed absurd. I shifted my attention from my relatively trivial loss to her colossal bereavement and did all I could to help her through an unimaginably difficult time.

When I finally did tell Alex about the ring, he wasn't nearly as upset as I had expected him to be. He looked at me in his Buddhist way to relax me and said, "It's only material. Don't worry about it." In the end, I hope that whoever kept that ring needed the money and put it to good use.

Being generous is the keystone of elegance. A generosity of spirit, a sincere concern for those around us, is what lies behind civility. Acting on that impulse can change the world.

I believe that with all my heart.

From my modeling days in Milan

(COURTESY OF THE AUTHOR)

What's Outside

*O*N ELEGANCE

There is a theme to much of the correspondence I have received from fans of *Real Housewives*. People seem troubled about whether elegance has any place in the world today, whether the old rules apply anymore. One book describes the situation this way: "This restless time is so varied, so quick in its changes, that it takes a mental trapeze artist to discover and accept its framework."

The truth is that I found this quote in *Better Than Beauty: A Guide to Charm,* a book that was originally published in 1938. I have reproduced these words here to demonstrate that elegance has always been a rare quality, a calm presence in the turmoil of everyday life.

Elegance is unmistakable—we all know it when we see it, but it is nearly impossible to define. Elegance is the way a woman carries herself, grace of movement, the warmth of her smile, the light in her eyes, the sheen of her hair, her distinctive style, the harmony of her manners, wit, and poise, an air of mystery, and her ability to engage anyone in conversation. And that's just for starters.

Princess Grace was the embodiment of elegance in my eyes. Her swanlike grace, flawless appearance, and remarkable polish made her one of the most admired women in the world—a true icon. My husband's father served as ambassador of Monaco for forty-three years. My husband, who knew Princess Grace from the time he was seventeen, always talks about her with great fondness and admiration. She was a beautiful woman of great character and compassion who had extraordinary style.

Elegance means handling all aspects of your life with self-confidence and aplomb. Elegance has no shelf life or expiration date. Elegance is a quality that does not age. It is an aura that enchants those around you, regardless of your stage in life or your station.

> I would not have written this book if I did not believe elegance could be acquired.

I hope you do not find my description of elegance daunting. I would not have written this book if I did not believe elegance could be acquired. My aim is to help you achieve elegance—or at least know how to fake it until it comes naturally.

12 THINGS ELEGANT PEOPLE ARE NEVER SEEN DOING

1. Exposing the sole of a shoe when crossing legs for all to see.
2. Yawning—try to stifle a yawn whenever possible, but always cover your mouth in public.
3. Chewing gum—to keep your mouth fresh, carry mints.
4. Speaking loudly—speaking softly instead will draw people closer and won't be inconsiderate.
5. Displaying nervous habits (biting nails, cracking knuckles, leg or foot jiggling)—avoid gestures that reveal a lack of ease.
6. Staring—glancing works better.
7. Pointing—never make someone else feel self-conscious.
8. Losing their temper—take three deep breaths.
9. Applying makeup in public—please, go to the ladies' room. But a quick check in the compact for lipstick is okay.
10. Combing or brushing hair in public—never!
11. Being negative—being a pessimist is unattractive and brings everyone down.
12. Putting on airs—a gracious person is never pretentious or snobbish.

Today, we have so many choices about how to live and how we want to look. There are even several types of elegance, including classic, refined, relaxed, modern, or slightly bohemian. It just so happens that the word *elegance* is derived from the Latin *eligere*, which means "to select." To be elegant, you should have a strong sense of self. You have to know yourself well enough to make sophisticated choices about how you look, behave, and live that express who you are and reflect the best of you.

*C*HIC IS CHARM MADE VISIBLE

Chic is a French word for which there is not an English transla-
tion. The best we can come up with is another French phrase. We
say that a woman has a certain *je ne sais quoi,* literally, "I don't
know what," but it is something special.

According to Genevieve Antoine Dariaux, who was the director of the couture house Nina Ricci for many years, chic is "the
essence of casual refinement, which is a little less studied than
elegance and a little more in-
tellectual. . . . It is a gift of the
gods and has no relationship
to beauty or wealth."

> A chic woman
> draws attention to
> herself without ever
> being obvious.

When a woman is chic, it
does not mean she is dressed
to the nines, all coordinated
to perfection. You can spend
hours getting ready to go out,
but if you are chic, you never appear to have done so. Your look
must seem to have just happened.

Chic requires a sense of proportion, discrimination, simplicity,
and restraint. It involves so much more than dressing well. A chic
woman knows who she is and communicates it with her look. She
knows how to highlight her good qualities and play down her faults.
A chic woman must not seem too conscious of what she is wearing.

Chic is what counts in our informal world. You can be chic
regardless of your budget or whatever your age. It's about the way
you put things together. It's about not letting the clothes wear
you. Haven't you noticed people who roll up their cuffs with flair,
belt a sweater a certain way, turn up a collar, wear striking colors
in unexpected combinations, always wear an eye-catching piece

of jewelry, know how to use scarves in elegant ways? A chic woman draws attention to herself without ever being obvious.

$\mathcal{K}$NOCKING THEM DEAD

I do not have to tell you how important first impressions are. We judge and are judged in an instant. What people notice first about you is your posture, your eyes and smile, and for me, your shoes. I've learned you can tell a lot about people from their shoes. When you have time to take care of your shoes, you have time for everything else.

These characteristics send a subliminal message about your character and your mood. In combination they say a great deal about who you are. They can make you appealing and approachable or unattractive and off-putting. You don't have to be beautiful to be alluring. What you need is vitality. If you carry yourself beautifully with assurance, have sparkling eyes, a glowing smile, everyone wants to get close to you. You know when certain people enter a room. You want to be near them, because they have that extra something.

$\mathcal{M}$OVING THROUGH THE WORLD

Carriage has always been an indication of good breeding. For centuries, well-brought-up young women walked erect, balancing books on their heads to improve their posture. Though the emphasis on carriage has faded today, good posture still communicates elegance and self-possession. If I weren't sitting erect in church in my little Sunday dress, the dreaded hand reached over to give me a reminder slap. My mother had the longest arms ever.

The way you hold and carry yourself reveals so very much about how you feel about yourself and others. Standing up straight makes you appear confident, optimistic, and slimmer. If you slouch, you are more likely to look old, sloppy, exhausted, discouraged, and frumpy. Throw your shoulders back and smile. Everything, including your clothes, will look better. Just think *tall*.

The way you walk also telegraphs a lot about you. Try to have bounce and lightness in your step and avoid shuffling or stomping. Glide! When you walk, look straight ahead, glancing down for the occasional curb or crack in the pavement.

When you sit in a chair, don't collapse or fall into it. Lower yourself gently into your seat. When seated, be comfortable. You don't have to sit ramrod straight, but you shouldn't slump or slouch either.

As a beauty contestant in the Miss Connecticut pageant, I realized I had many tricks to learn. I nervously watched the preliminary interviews as I waited for my turn. I realized that the way each girl sat, particularly the way she placed her legs, revealed a lot about her. The most flattering position was when both feet were placed side by side and then tucked off to one side.

From watching others walk on those pageant runways and doing so myself, I realized that the way you move must appear effortless. Your posture should be relaxed and supple, not artificial and self-conscious. Your aim is not to distract people's attention with awkward, sloppy movements. When you hold yourself in a stiff way, you display your tension and anxiety for all to read. Notice if your jaw or your hands are clenched. Rigidity is a dead giveaway that you are uncomfortable. If you find your body tensing up in a social situation, take a few deep breaths and smile. The pageant girls used to put Vaseline on their teeth so they could hold their smiles longer. I wish someone had told me sooner. I felt as if I had lockjaw.

Now and then, you should take stock of the message your body language is sending. If you have a frown on your face, you are slouching, and your arms are folded tightly in front of you, it's not a pleasant sight. If you turn your back on someone, twist your legs away from someone when seated, rest your head in your hand, or look distracted, you will not seem open and accessible. These postures and gestures send a negative message. Consider the difference if you sit up, smile, are relaxed, have a bounce to your step, lean in slightly when you talk, make eye contact, nod in agreement. It makes a big difference!

A CRASH COURSE IN WALKING IN JIMMY CHOOS

When I was a teenager, I was self-conscious about being tall, and all the boys were shorter than I. I once bought a pair of high-heeled boots with every intention of wearing them, because I loved heels. When I went to put them on, turning round and round in the mirror, I felt too tall to leave the house. I proceeded to whip out my father's handsaw to cut the heels down. Not a good idea.

My mother always said to me, "You'll be so happy when you grow up to be tall."

She was right. My mother always left the house in hose and high heels. She's probably one of the most elegant women I know. She's a natural.

Even though I am five feet ten inches tall, I adore high heels—the higher the better—so luncheons, parties, business meetings, dinners out, evenings at the theater, are all occasions for high heels. The key is comfort. You can definitely find the slipper that fits. If you really can't manage sky-high heels, find the highest ones you can handle comfortably. It will be worth the effort.

High heels are sexy. They will make you have a longer silhouette.

Anytime I want to look my best, I wear my Jimmy Choos, because they are classic. But you don't want to spoil the effect by tottering on your stilettos. Taking mincing steps or limping is not a very elegant way to move. Many of my friends put pads in their shoes to relieve the weight on the balls of their feet or wear a great-looking lower heel or flat and switch them for a sexier pair in the office.

I love wearing boots because they're easy to walk in and look great. Also, when I have to race around town, I often wear ballet slippers to save wear and tear on my feet. If you are commuting to your office, you might want to leave a pair or two of high heels in the office and use a nice pair of flats or lower heels for coming and going. If you have to go with colleagues to a meeting, you could slip ballet slippers into your briefcase or handbag for afterward. Leave your sneakers at the gym.

A good fit is essential. Who needs blisters and aching feet to put a damper on your good time? The higher the heel, the more money you should invest in the shoe. Good shoes are worth the investment. Good design is essential for balance and comfort. If you find a brand or a design that works for you, stick with it. Buy it in every color. There is nothing wrong with wearing classic shoes for a long time if they are well maintained. You can have them resoled a number of times to extend their life. In fact, some leathers become more beautiful with use and develop a burnished patina that makes a statement about quality. I have boots I bought years ago in Milan when I shopped Via Montenapoleone, one of the oldest cobblestone streets in the city.

There are so many danger zones in a city—gratings and cracks in the sidewalks, marble lobbies or plazas—that walking in high heels can be hazardous. You have to become confident about walking in heels, and the only way you can do that is to practice when you get a new pair. I wear new shoes in the house to break them in for the street.

- You don't want to wobble, teeter, or stomp. Put one foot in front of the other as if you're walking a straight line.
- Don't look at your feet as you walk. Scan the terrain ahead of you.
- Don't throw your body out of alignment by pitching forward to compensate.
- Keep your back straight, hold your stomach in and your chin up.
- Take a normal-length stride.

Glide, ladies, glide your way up and down those steps like a goddess.

The Foundation of Good Looks

Good grooming is essential for making a good impression. All the personality and fine clothing in the world will not compensate for looking unkempt and sloppy. The basics really do matter. You should start with a full-length mirror and an unforgiving magnifying mirror for your face. Never leave your house or greet guests without checking both. I always have a mirror at the entrance to our homes so I can check myself before going out to make certain I am together and so guests can pause before entering. That's why I love mirrors in elevators.

*H*EAD-TO-TOE GROOMING

- Hair is clean, shining, and neat—using a shine spray is a must if your hair is dull.
- Eyebrows are well shaped, without stray hairs. Shape them with your finger in a pinch. If you don't have an eyebrow brush, get one. Your eyebrows are the frame of your face.
- Skin is a clear and a healthy base for makeup.
- Teeth are white and gums healthy.
- Breath is sweet. There is nothing worse than bad breath.
- Makeup is subtle and well blended—no foundation on the neck or clothing, no running mascara.
- Hands and nails are well taken care of—no chipped nail polish or ragged cuticles, please.
- Legs are smooth—I love tanning creams if my legs are bare.
- Feet are well cared for—no calluses or blisters.
- Clothing is clean, pressed, and spot-free.
- Lingerie is visible only if you want it to be.
- No runs or snags are in stockings.
- Shoes are clean, without run-down heels or scuffed tips.
- Handbags or totes complement the outfit and are of pleasing proportion.
- Fragrance is light and fresh during the day, a bit more intense in the evening, but never overwhelming.

Being well groomed is a matter of habit. It primarily involves maintenance. Before you put away an article of clothing, examine it carefully. Does it need to be washed or dry-cleaned? Is a button loose or a hem torn? If so, leave it out to repair the next day. In a pinch, I use the Tide stick eraser for my clothes, and if I discover my shoes are a bit scuffed, I use a damp cloth. Don't just kick your shoes off into a corner or hang your purse on a doorknob at the end of the day. Store them carefully in your closet. Treat them like an investment.

*Y*OU CAN'T LOOK GOOD
*I*F YOU DON'T FEEL GOOD

No matter how much effort you put into your appearance, it just won't work unless you start by taking care of yourself. Our lives seem to get busier as we multitask our way through each day. We wear so many hats—wife, mother, social director, chef, concierge, fund-raiser, fashion consultant—in addition to any job we might have. Sometimes I can't believe how much we have to balance and the pace at which we live. When we get caught up in the whirlwind of our lives, it's easy to forget the basic things we need to do to promote our own health and well-being. Slow down. If you don't take care of yourself, nobody else will.

Good looks and an upbeat attitude depend on a good night's sleep, eating smart, and daily exercise. I know there aren't enough hours in a day, but you have to pay attention to these essentials. All three are important to keep your energy high, your eyes sparkling, and your tail wagging. These aren't things you can do now and then to feel good. They have to be part of your routine. Making healthy choices has to become a habit, as necessary as brushing your teeth in the morning. Once you start taking good care of yourself, you'll feel so great you'll never want to return to your former ways. And if you lapse—as we all do—you'll be able to get right back on track.

Skimping on sleep is never good for you, but it happens. A minimum of seven to eight hours of sleep a night is necessary for most of us to restore our mind and body after a busy day, although some people can get away with less. Not me. A good night's sleep will help you avoid getting sick and

> ## Every day you open your eyes is a good day.

speed up your recuperation if you are. Your mood depends a lot on how much you sleep. I try to get seven or eight solid hours per night. Try to hit the sheets free of worry, arguments, and stress. Every day you open your eyes is a good day.

If you're not getting enough sleep, you will think less clearly, have difficulty concentrating, be slower, and have a harder time remembering things. Worst of all, too little sleep can affect your metabolism, causing you to gain weight. Hormones released while you sleep affect how your body uses energy. Studies have found that the less people sleep, the more they are likely to be overweight. If that isn't a persuasive argument for getting more sleep, I don't know what is.

EATING IS A CELEBRATION

In the United States, we so often eat whatever is convenient "on the go." If you sit down and take the time to enjoy what you eat, you will find your food more satisfying. Meals should be a social event. Get your family to sit down together to eat more often. You will all be healthier and happier.

Eating is sensual, a celebration. I enjoy everything that goes into preparing a good meal. It starts with deciding what to eat and shopping for it at the market.

It's so much fun to prepare the food with friends or the kids. Setting a beautiful table creates a perfect way to present a good meal. But what is most important is bringing family and friends together to enjoy each other, their conversation, and the meal. The meal doesn't have to be haute cuisine. Fresh, simple food will do the trick. Of course, Europeans usually enjoy wine with their meals to awaken their taste buds, to heighten the experience, and to create a convivial atmosphere. It's all about savoring the food and the company in a civilized way.

I've always been charmed by the European custom of serving a complimentary dish before you have even ordered at a restaurant. In Italy, it might be prosciutto, cheese, pickled vegetables, or olives. In France, an amuse-bouche, a little treat whipped up by the chef, is often served with drinks. It's so generous and welcoming.

In the United States, meals are too large. In Europe, portions are much smaller, and going back for more is unheard of. If you find it difficult to control how much you eat, use smaller plates. The optical illusion really will trick you into perceiving the portions as bigger.

Eat a rainbow.

For me, good nutrition is a matter of common sense and listening to what your body tells you. There are hundreds, if not thousands, of diet books out there. I like the Blood Type Diet, because I think that each person actually is a carnivore or an herbivore. Since I'm Type O, I need more meat and my body craves it.

Eat a rainbow. My rule of thumb is to eat foods of many colors. Think about it. White food is usually not great if you have any weight concerns—sugar, flour, pasta, rice, potatoes, white bread. My friend Honeychile used to say, "If you eat the bread, skip the wine. If you drink the wine, skip the bread. It's one or the other—the wine or the bread." I personally choose the wine.

If you select primarily from the rainbow of color fruits and vegetables have to offer, you will provide your body with the nutrition it needs to stay healthy. I limit how much red meat I eat and concentrate my protein in cheese, chicken, pork, fish, and seafood. I also stick with whole-grain breads because they digest more slowly. I don't need to tell you to avoid fried foods and sweets.

I try not to eat anything that comes in a package. Who needs preservatives, chemicals, salt, corn syrup, and who knows what else? Eating fresh food is much better for you—and the difference in taste is a treat. If you shop the perimeter of your supermarket, rather than up and down the aisles, you will find the fresh foods— produce, meat and fish, eggs, dairy products, even fresh baked goods, just about everything you need for a nutritious diet. Never go to the supermarket hungry. Those middle aisles will be too hard to resist.

> **I try not to eat anything that comes in a package.**

Don't try to go too long without eating. You should eat when you are hungry. A number of small meals is a better way to go. Otherwise, your body will crave all sorts of things for a quick fix. Europeans rarely snack. My husband always says those familiar words: "Don't eat before you go out; you'll ruin your dinner." But I know that if I leave the house hungry, I will eat more when we go out for dinner. And eating a big meal late in the evening isn't good for you. So have a light snack in the late afternoon. It will curb your hunger and keep you from eating like a bear at dinner.

If you are going to eat when you are hungry, that means knowing that what you are feeling is hunger rather than a craving or an emotionally driven appetite. My luck is that I can't eat when I'm upset. Others overeat when they are.

> **Remember: Drink twenty minutes before or after a meal.**

Make sure you have healthy snacks around—with an emphasis on protein. Protein takes longer to digest and will fill you up longer. Low-fat yogurt, string cheese, a few nuts, or a hard-boiled egg are good options. If you crave sweets, a piece of fruit or some berries might satisfy your sweet tooth. Xochai dark chocolate does it for me.

Try not to drink when eating—not even water—because digestion begins in the mouth.

Remember: Drink twenty minutes before or after a meal. People have a tendency to wash their food down with a beverage rather than chewing each bite thoroughly and allowing enzymes to begin their work. Chewing your food in this way will taste better, too. I'll never forget this fact. It was drummed into my head at a monastic Austrian Spa.

> # Don't let go of the vision of yourself.

I often joined my husband and friends for "cures" at European spas. They believe it is important to cleanse the system once a year, and I would go along for the ride. This particular spa was very strict. We were to fast and consume a severely limited diet. Pavarotti was undergoing the "cure" there at the same time we were. He had his own elevator to carry his considerable bulk up and down!

On the first day, we sat in the dining room for a spare lunch. We were instructed to chew our yogurt and even our water forty times. We found it so hilarious that we couldn't look at each other for fear we would burst out laughing. Who knows how our militaristic guards—or should I say friendly spa attendants—would have responded? To this day, I giggle when I think of us chewing water.

Despite this rigorous training, I still love a good glass of red wine with my meals. Sipping a little wine is better than drinking diet Coke, fruit juices, and even water. Washing your food down delays digestion. If you want to drink, this is what happy hours and cocktail parties are for.

These are my simple rules for eating well. Food is one of the great pleasures in life. Learn to enjoy eating the right way, and it will be evident in your good skin, figure, and radiant health.

*Y*OU'VE GOT TO MOVE

You have to expend energy to have energy, not to mention the positive hormonal effects exercise has on the brain. I always say don't let go of the vision of yourself. It takes exercise to stay in shape, particularly as we age.

During my Connecticut days, I briefly taught an exercise class for the elderly at the request of nurses and nurses' aides. It was my Jane Fonda moment—leg warmers, tights, high-cut leotard, head band to hold back my big hair. Remember that look?

When I first moved to New York to model, I was walking all over the city from appointment to appointment rather than driving as I had done in Connecticut. This helped me considerably to lose weight. One day, after a modeling "go-see," I ran into an extremely thin model and asked her how she did it. "Have you seen the prices of food in New York?" was her response. I realized that she was starving, not dieting.

Actually, in those days I couldn't afford to go to restaurants, so I understood what she was talking about. I lived on a tight budget, and I really didn't cook for myself. I lived on eggs, yogurt, bananas, and an occasional congratulatory slice of pizza when I wasn't being taken out to dinner.

When I went to Europe, the modeling agencies in Europe told me I had to lose fifteen pounds. I had lost weight in New York and was already thin but not thin enough. I had no intention of losing more weight. At the time, exercise wasn't that popular in Italy. No one seemed to exercise at all, but the Italians were tiny by any standard. I joined a gym and decided that I had to watch what I ate. The diet that has served me well over the years is Fit for Life. It boils down to having meat or potatoes but not both.

After I married Alex and returned to the United States, I got into the Lotte Berk Method—which is a combination of dance and isometric exercise. It is militaristic and painful, but I wanted to look good, and a lot of my friends were doing it. When I was pregnant with Victoria, I worked out until three days before she was born. The other women couldn't believe I was still working out. They were certain the baby was going to shoot out of me as we did squats. I had a goal of not gaining more than thirty pounds during my pregnancy, and I was intent on keeping it.

Since I've had my children, I like to change up my exercise routine and do a variety of exercises, better known as crosstraining. Sometimes I work out at the gym with weights and do aerobics on an elliptical machine two or, if I'm lucky, three times a week. On weekends, I do Pilates, play tennis, ride a bike, and take long walks.

When I can't get to the gym, I do a yoga routine every morning for ten minutes. I love to start my day this way, because it gets my circulation going and stretches me out. I think being limber keeps you young. I begin with the Salutation to the Sun, a series of twelve postures that alternate backward and forward bending to flex and stretch the spinal column. I follow that with a headstand, considered one of the most powerful yoga positions because it increases circulation to the brain and the face most importantly, and that improves your mind and increases your vitality. My entire routine takes ten minutes.

Yoga has played a big role in my life. It saved me from the

effects of a traumatic experience. I was driving with my children, who were then four and two, from a tea party to celebrate Elle Macpherson's son's birthday in Gstaad. It was dusk—about six in the evening—just at the point when the roads freeze. I was driving carefully down a winding mountain road when my car just drifted toward the edge. There was nothing I could do to correct it. It all happened in slow motion. There wasn't a fence or barricade to prevent my Range Rover from slipping over the side into a sheer drop. The car flipped over three times down the slope. With each revolution, the roof hit the snow with a thundering *thumpf*. I thought surely all of us would die.

We landed at the bottom of the mountain, hanging upside down, held in our seats by our seat belts, with steam hissing from the car. As we rolled down the mountainside, there was nothing in the way—not a single tree or boulder obstructed our path. We crawled out in a foot of snow when the car came to rest at the foot of the mountain, having just missed a dairy barn. Miraculously, we escaped unscathed.

The emotional aftermath of that terrifying accident led me to find yoga. I needed to center myself and to be able to breath easily again. I studied with Deepak Chopra, a brilliant and spiritual man. His teaching inspired me, and the practice of yoga restored my strength and calm. Yoga has become an integral part of my life.

Being mindful of your breath has a calming influence. Deep breathing is a fundamental technique in the practice of yoga, and a wonderful way to reconnect with your life force anytime, anyplace. You can do it sitting up or lying on your back. Our normal breath tends to be shallow and uses only the top part of our lungs. The technique of deep breathing uses the entire capacity of the lungs. Think of the way babies breathe, their stomachs going in and out with each breath.

- ❧ Breathe through your nose, first into your diaphragm, filling your stomach with air.
- ❧ Continue to inhale and fill your chest with air, expanding it.
- ❧ Lift your shoulder slightly to pull the last bit of oxygen into your lungs.
- ❧ As you exhale through your nose, relax your shoulders, soften your chest, and pull your stomach in as far as you can at the end of the inhalation.
- ❧ Do this to a count of seven in, seven out. It's a great way to relax.

Yoga is great, but it's not enough on its own. It's a good idea to add aerobics to your schedule, too, if you can. Fifteen to thirty minutes twice a week should do the trick. The idea is to break a sweat and to get your heart pumping. I work out on an elliptical machine because it's easier on the joints and generally better for the body.

If all else fails, walk—every day. New Yorkers are used to walking at top speed around the city in our rush to go places and get things done. If you don't live in a city and find yourself sitting behind the wheel of a car, get out there and walk. Enjoy the neighborhood or the countryside alone or with a friend. And if you have a dog, your pet will love it too.

*H*AIR AND MAKEUP

Wouldn't it be great to have people to do your hair and makeup every day? I certainly enjoyed it when I was on Italian TV. I've heard that two stylists worked on Princess Diana's hair simultaneously to cut down on blow-drying time. Bliss! Unfortunately, there is no "hair and makeup" for *The Real Housewives of New York City*. Each of us is responsible for how we look when we shoot. When we are not filming real scenes in normal lighting, we have to sit down for interviews to explain story lines. That's when it's hard to get makeup right, because of the stage lighting. I'm good with makeup from my modeling days, but I'm not a makeup artist. If I had one wish—after world peace and an end to poverty—it would be for a hair and makeup person every single day.

Getting fake eyelashes in Milan
(COURTESY OF THE AUTHOR)

Since I don't have time to primp every day, I do best with a look that is natural. It simply isn't practical for most of us to have high-maintenance hairstyles, and at the same time, it's also not stylish.

I think it's a mistake to let your hair and makeup call too much attention to itself.

Your aim is to frame your face and highlight your best features in a subtle, flattering way. Some people go for high drama, which can be glamorous at night, but dramatic makeup every day gets tired and can make you look older. What was at first remarkable can seem too artificial. The same goes for the no-makeup look. After a certain age, you have to highlight your best qualities— brows, eyes, lips—so you look natural, but not like a plain Jane.

ON EYEBROWS

Pay attention to your eyebrows. They frame your eyes and help to define the shape of your face. It is well worth having a professional shape your eyebrows. Then you can maintain the shape yourself with light plucking whenever you see a stray hair.

In big cities, there are salons dedicated to brows. Facialists are often trained to work on eyebrows. Beauty salons and manicure shops that offer waxing will often be able to help. Just be certain that the natural shape of your eyebrows is honored and that your eyebrows aren't plucked unnaturally thin. Think Brooke Shields.

Some people wax their eyebrows, but do be careful, because the skin on your eyelids is very sensitive. I once had half an eyebrow removed by mistake.

Some people's eyebrows are too dark, while others' are so fair they disappear. If you color your hair, you will want to coordinate the color of your eyebrows. A hair colorist will tint your eyebrows when your hair is being done. ***Never do this on your own.***

Having beautiful, well-shaped eyebrows makes your whole face.

YOUR CROWNING GLORY

Hair is not about following every trend or changing your look; it's about knowing yourself and working with what works best for you. I can't tell you how many times I've made the mistake of letting a hairdresser decide how I should look. My reaction goes from tears to anger—I'm sure you've been there. That's why going to the hairdresser with an idea of what you want and what looks good for your face will protect you from hearing those dreaded words: "Don't worry. It will grow back." I used to wear my hair long, but it seems the older I got, the shorter I wore my hair. I think it suits my face better because it accents my cheekbones. My favorite cut was the blunt cut I had in Milan. Though my hair is layered now, it's a length that works for me. The secret to having sensational hair is a good cut that requires a minimal amount of care for your type of hair. It's all in the cut, and the shape that works for your face.

When it comes to hair color, you also want to go for a natural look. And just as you need a professional stylist to cut your hair, so, too, should you have your hair colored professionally when you want to change it. Don't ever try to do it on your own. A colorist is trained to know what will work best with your complexion and eyes so that your look is harmonious. Trust me: It's worth paying for. If you look at hair in its natural state, you will see that it is not a uniform color. (Just look at your kids' hair.) Since it begins with various shades, your hair will absorb the dye differently strand by strand. And that is good. A head of hair that is a solid color looks over-dyed by the hand of an amateur. That's why it's important to go to the hairdresser.

If you have your color done once professionally, they will

often tell you what colors they mixed to achieve it. Friends of mine always say that they are traveling and love the color so much that they want to know how to reproduce it while they are away. If you have the formula, you can go to a more modest salon to do it. If you are a regular customer at a high-end salon, colorists will often send product to you wherever you are so that a local salon can keep your hair looking great.

I do think coloring your hair as you age will erase some years. Hair tends to dull as you age, and coloring it can make it look richer. Adding the illusion of sheen is one of the reasons people opt for lowlights and highlights. That is not to say that everyone should go this route. Some women's hair turns a beautiful snowy white that is almost platinum, others a striking salt and pepper that gives them a stately elegance. A consultation with a colorist can help you to decide the best way to keep your hair your crowning glory. I go for styling and highlights.

We are fortunate to have so many wonderful hair products available for our use at reasonable prices. At the price clubs, you can find sophisticated products that have been supersized. Change your shampoo and conditioner monthly, because a residue can build up that a new product will wash away. Because of my hair type, washing it every other day does the trick. My daughter and I love to experiment with different brands. We never cease to be amazed at the range of the selection and the high quality of what is available. Just be certain you use a product designed to protect your hair as you style it. I like to use a silicon flatiron to smooth hair at the end of styling, because it adds shine.

*T*HE RARE BAD HAIR DAY

On a bad hair day, I use a little Pucci scarf, the size of a handker-chief, which I knot at the back of my head. My break-dancing son would call it do-rag style. I call it *my* style. Princess Grace and Jackie O. did it—why can't we?

In many instances, a hat does the trick. Slicking back your hair or putting it up and hiding it under a great hat is the best way to go. In the summer, it can be a glamorous straw hat or a wind-blown scarf, in the winter, a beret or colorful cap into which you can tuck your hair. Be ready to draw attention.

If you are not a hat person, go to a department store, try on a few, and become one.

If you have your grooming rituals under control, you should not face a bad hair day often, but they are unavoidable every now and then. A late night out followed by a breakfast date, getting soaked in a sudden rainstorm, having to meet someone for drinks after a workout, all require emergency measures. If it has some length, you can put it in a ponytail or twist it up. If you are lucky enough to have a style you can shape with your fingers, you can just wash or wet your hair and let it dry.

Satin pillows, which you can buy in any linen store, will help you avoid "bed head." They also prevent facial wrinkles. (I like the idea though I haven't tried one.)

$\mathscr{K}$EEP IT SUBTLE

I believe that makeup should be kept to a minimum. Minimal makeup—or at least makeup that appears to be minimal—will make you look younger. What you want to achieve is a fresh, healthy, glowing face with emphasis on your finest features. If you have gorgeous eyes, play them up with eyeliner and mascara. Your cheekbones will be even more striking with a proper application of blush. If your lips are full and luscious, you might select a sexy red lipstick and go with less eye makeup. If your lips are less than luscious, play up your eyes. If you are known for your smile, you will want to choose a color that makes your teeth look even whiter. It's all a question of balance.

Most of us do need to use a foundation to even out our skin tone. Some of us can get away with a sheer foundation, while others need more coverage. There is a staggering array of choices—oil-free, super-rich, mousses, creams in a compact or a stick, tinted moisturizers, liquid powders—you have to find what works best for you. Having had acne as a teenager, I tend to use products that are oil-free.

$\mathscr{M}$AKEUP ARTISTS ON CALL

When I was modeling in New York, I would sometimes stop at a department store before a date to have my makeup done. Every makeup counter has professional makeup artists who apply makeup for free to sell their products. Even high-end pharmacies and some big drugstore chains offer the service. If you are planning a special evening, why not have your face made up by a professional?

*W*HAT TO DO WITH A SHINY FACE

Though we all want shiny hair, a shiny face is a definite problem. My secret weapon is blotting paper. It's an old-fashioned remedy that you can find in any pharmacy. Blotting paper is powdered tissue that comes in small pads. Simply tear off a sheet and pat your face. The powder and the porous paper will absorb the excessive oil from your skin.

Since I have a T-zone face, with oily skin across my forehead and down my nose, I don't leave home without blotting paper tucked into my makeup bag. I prefer using blotting paper to powder, which can get caked.

One of the best ways to learn about makeup is to shop the makeup departments on the ground floor of most department stores. Most of the time, those makeup artists are standing there just waiting for you to ask them for help. Take advantage of the opportunity to have a complimentary makeup session in a department store's cosmetic department. You will get an education that goes beyond the product line being sold at the counter. You will discover what sort of foundation and blusher are right for your skin. You will learn how to apply the makeup and how to do your eyes and lips. You

> **Take advantage of the opportunity to have a complimentary makeup session in a department store's cosmetic department.**

can try products that you might not be able to afford otherwise. You are not obligated to buy anything. So hit Chanel, MAC, Bobbi Brown, Lancôme, Clarins . . . the list goes on.

I would suggest that you tip the artist if you do not buy anything, but you'll often find one of the products so flattering that you will want to add it to your makeup bag. How much to tip depends on where you live. Keep in mind that a good makeup person costs at least $150 an hour. Of course, a tip is not required, but it's cheaper than buying all the products. Tipping made me friends at a number of counters, and I was always welcomed back.

> You should have a set of makeup for winter and one for summer if you don't live in the Sunbelt.

If you have a makeup session and your goal is to find daytime makeup, tell the stylist. If the makeup artist is putting it on with a trowel and using bright colors, don't hesitate to repeat that you want a face you can wear every day. During the day, when natural light is strong, too much makeup is obvious. I use bronzing powder as a blush to give my face a sun-kissed look. At night, it's fun to go a little wild and use more dramatic colors. You should have a set of makeup for winter and one for summer if you don't live in the Sunbelt. If you get some color in the summer, you will definitely need to change the color of your foundation. But even if you stay the same shade all year, you will want to change the color of your lipstick and blush to coordinate with seasonal hues of your clothes.

ℋAIR AND MAKEUP FAUX PAS

1. **Hair that needs to be washed**—good grooming requires cleanliness. In an emergency, cover up with a hat or scarf.

2. **Split ends or hair frizzled with dryness**—regular trims and deep conditioning treatments will take care of these problems.

3. **Visible roots**—establish an upkeep regimen that you follow. Make the dates on your calendar.

4. **Helmet head from too much hair spray or gel**—hair has to move to be alluring.

5. **Hair color not found in nature**—if you want to play with vibrant colors, incorporate them into your wardrobe.

6. **Foundations that doesn't match your skin tone and stops at your jaw**—don't try to change the skin you are in. Select a foundation that complements it and makes it richer. The idea is to look natural, not two-toned.

7. **Blush that is too vivid and not blended**—the clown face is never elegant. I prefer powders, myself.

8. **A shiny face**—blotting paper to the rescue.

9. **Lip pencil applied outside your lips**—put lip liner inside your lips. Don't try to create an optical illusion by doing the fake lip.

10. **Lipstick on your teeth**—always check your teeth after applying lipstick.

11. **Raccoon eyes**—dark circles under your eyes from runny mascara defeats the purpose. Concealer to the rescue.

12. **Self-tanners on the face**—I don't recommend this, unless it's summer and it matches your body.

$\mathscr{N}$EVER LEAVE A DEPARTMENT STORE WITHOUT A SAMPLE

My good friend Princess Hohenlohe used to leave a department store with bags of samples. She could well afford to buy anything she wanted. She just had fun charming the people behind the counters, who showered her with samples—from Chanel to La Mer. Don't forget that department stores give away complimentary samples of almost every brand they carry.

Don't be shy. The sample products are made to be given away. You can just say, "I've heard so many wonderful things about your night cream. Do you have a sample I could try?" Or "I read in a magazine—was it *Vogue* or *InStyle*?—that your new foundation has a terrific texture and great coverage. Do you have a sample I could try?" Or "Do you have anything to help me cover up these bags under my eyes? I'd love to try a sample."

> ## Stay away from waterproof mascara.

Stay away from waterproof mascara. It is harsh and not great for your eyelashes. Removing it can cause your eyelashes to break, and the last thing we want to do is lose eyelashes.

I use an array of different products. I adore Chanel lipstick because it's long-lasting. Lancome makes the best mascara. It doesn't smear or run. Try all kinds of makeup, and don't be afraid to change. Your makeup does not have to be wildly expensive. You can find wonderful cosmetics in the drugstore. Find it and stick with it—day and night, summer and winter.

WHAT YOU'LL FIND IN MY MAKEUP BAG

- Liquid foundation: Armani #7
- Bronzing powder: Chanel
- Eyebrow pencil: Chanel
- Mascara: Lancôme
- Eyeliner pencil: Chanel
- Lip gloss: Chanel

A MONTHLY AT-HOME SPA

I treat myself to a deep cleansing facial once a month. If you can treat yourself to a professional facial, consider the experience a chance to relax while you restore your skin, and to rid it of all the pollution it absorbs from the atmosphere. If a spa treatment is beyond your budget, you can have the same experience at home. Create the right ambience for your facial. Low lights, scented candles, soft, restful music. Yummy. Lock your door. I can't tell you how many times I've scared my own kids with a green facial mask.

There are hundreds of products available in your drugstore and supermarket designed to treat all varieties of skin. You should select a deep-cleansing mask for your skin type, or a clarifying, moisturizing, peeling, or cooling mask, depending on your needs.

SIMPLE AT-HOME FACIAL

1. Clean your face gently with a cleanser, cream, or mild soap. Rinse with warm water.

2. You can begin by steaming your skin over a bowl of hot water. Put boiling water in a bowl. Lean over the bowl and put a towel over your head to trap the steam. Just be careful that the water is not too hot and your face is not too close to the bowl. You want to steam, not blister.

3. Once you have steamed your face, exfoliate gently with grains for that purpose or a slightly rough cloth.

4. Apply the mask of your choice. Lie down in the luxurious atmosphere you have created for yourself. Set a timer for ten or fifteen minutes, depending on the mask, so you don't have to worry about it. If you're like me, one of the kids will interrupt anyway.

5. When the timer rings, gently clean off the mask with warm water.

6. Rinse with cool water and feel how smooth your skin is.

7. The whole process should not take more than forty-five minutes. Regardless of how busy you are, you can carve this time out for yourself once a month.

KEEPING UP YOUR APPEARANCE

Being well groomed requires regular maintenance. If you follow a routine, all this maintenance will become second nature, and you will be ready to go out on the town at a moment's notice. Taking good care of yourself will give you the energy and the desire to take care of everyone who depends on you.

I view taking care of my appearance as a chance to pamper myself. We are all so busy that making quiet time for ourselves has become a necessity. Creating a ritual around regular grooming activities will do a lot more than just improve how you look. You can make this a sensual experience, with fluffy towels, scented soaps, creams, shampoos, conditioners.

There are many things you can do at your at-home spa, including cellulite treatments, intensive hand and foot treatments, and super-conditioning for your hair. And there is nothing like a long soak in a bath with fragrant oils to moisturize your skin.

> I view taking care of my appearance as a chance to pamper myself.

Every once in a while, I treat myself to a full body massage at a spa. You can also have a masseuse come to your home. There's nothing better than than just throwing on a warm, comfy robe after a relaxing massage. There are so many massage techniques that target different problems—from muscle tension to toxin release, from cellulite reduction to pain relief. I love them all! If you buy massage oil, I'm sure your boyfriend or husband would enjoy giving you a massage—in fact, it's probably a fantasy of his.

*P*ERFUME

An alluring woman is often remembered for her fragrance. How we smell is an essential part of sex appeal and the hidden language of attraction. The right perfume or cologne will create an irresistible aura around you. It has to work with your biggest organ—your skin.

Finding a signature scent can be a project. Perfume is so personal. The same scent works differently on different people. Try many perfumes and test them with friends, husbands, and boy-friends. Estée Lauder, who had what is known in the industry as a "nose," used to say that she would look at people's eyes when they smelled a new perfume she was testing. If the perfume was right, their eyes would light up. When you see that lift in the eyes of others, you have hit the jackpot!

Walking through the ground floor of a department store has become either a tantalizing experience or one you want to run from—with so many offers of a trial spray or sample. Talking with the salespeople will give you a quick education on the vocabulary of perfume. Don't attempt to test too many scents in a visit, because you will not be able to distinguish one scent from another. Ask for samples and live with it for a day or two. Avoid scents that are too musky or manly—and please stay away from scents that make you smell like a canned fruit salad.

I have a scent for day and one for night. Of course, the day-time fragrance should be lighter. At night, perfume can be richer, with more depth. I recommend having winter and summer scents, too, just as you have different makeup colors for the two seasons. The humidity in the air changes the effect of perfume, so you'll want light notes for the summer.

I use Jo Malone's Grapefruit for day—it's so fresh—and Fracas for an air of mystery at night.

Proceed with caution when you use perfume. You don't want to overwhelm. Spray some perfume into the air and walk into the mist. That method will ensure an even scent from head to toe. I always add a touch by my ears for the cheek-to-cheek encounters. I do slip a small spray into my evening purse for touch-ups.

Now you are ready to present a great face to the world. After orchestrating your grooming and refining the hairstyle and makeup that works for you, you are now ready for the cherry on top—my favorite subject—fashion.

A glamorous shot at an Italian palazzo

(COURTESY OF THE AUTHOR)

Fashion and Style
3

*T*HERE IS ALWAYS AN EXCUSE TO SHOP

Appearing on *The Real Housewives of New York City* has been a bit of a fashion challenge. I have had to supplement my wardrobe with pieces that will work for the camera. Color has become an issue. For example, the tailored white shirt that is a staple for me would not vibrate on TV. Stripes that I would normally wear are not good for television. Don't misunderstand me—I'm not complaining. What is better than an excuse to go shopping?

You don't have to spend a lot of money to look great. I love fashion, because it allows me to be creative. There are so many colors, textures, and styles, and an infinite way to combine them. No matter what the occasion, I put thought into what I wear. I don't even come down to breakfast without slipping into a good-looking robe. I have defined my look and have a simple wardrobe to support it. I just update my basics with a few trendy pieces each season. I can pull myself together for any occasion in fifteen minutes or less. That's how easy it should be.

My husband prefers relaxed elegance. He likes it best when I dress informally—jeans, a white shirt, and a blazer—a look, he says, that is young. What he doesn't like is too much *décolleté*—a low-cut neckline—at least on me! We have to leave something to the imagination, darlings.

AUDREY HEPBURN FOR A NIGHT

I have to tell you a story about my favorite dream-come-true "shopping" experience. Roberto Gancia had introduced me to his dear friend Princess Hohenlohe, an American from the South who married a German prince. Honey, as she was known, was a colorful figure, beloved in all of Europe. Later, I'll tell you more about her and all she taught me. We were in Paris for the weekend and a friend offered us tickets to the opera. We hadn't packed for anything so grand. I was thrilled by the invitation, and Honey accepted effusively. "Of course we would love to go. How good of you." When I asked her later just what we were going to wear, she said, "Don't you worry, darling. Leave that to me."

We hopped into a car and flew through the wide boulevards of Paris and stopped on Avenue George V. When we pulled up in front of a stately home, she hopped out of the car and rang the bell. A voice responded over the intercom, asking who was there. "It's me, Honeychile. Hubert, let us up."

Hubert de Givenchy himself, tall and elegant, opened the door. The man who dressed Audrey Hepburn was stepping aside so we could enter his atelier. I was in awe. We had a wonderful afternoon trying on gowns as he dressed us from head to toe. Needless to say, we were the most splendid women in all of Paris that night, or at least we felt that way. My dress was long, black, and cut on a bias in silk crepe with a touch of white at the neck and a draping low back—kind of the flying nun in couture. I felt as if I were flying.

How you dress does make a powerful statement about who you are and who you want to be. Do you want to turn heads, get a promotion, look as if you are confident about giving that speech before the PTA, be a natural and elegant hostess, look as if you go to black-tie galas every night of the week? How you put together your look will make all the difference. That's the fun of fashion—you can be posh, comfy, sexy, preppy, stark, superfeminine, sporty, professional, trendy, bohemian, uptown, downtown, and anything else you can think of any day of the week. It depends on how you feel and what you want to say with your look.

Dress by Hubert Givenchy
(COURTESY OF THE AUTHOR)

ℐHE VALUE OF SIMPLICITY

My father used to say to me all the time, "The simple life is the best life." It took me a while to understand what that meant. He would say, "The reason it takes so long for you to get dressed is that you have too many things to choose from." I eventually learned that having less, of higher quality, is a better way to go.

You will get the best mileage from clothes that are simple and classic. Go for clean lines, fine fabrics, and the best fit you can find. Try to find a good tailor who can make alterations. Taking up a hem a few inches, shortening sleeves, removing or shaving shoulder pads can change the look of a garment. A good fit telegraphs quality. It is worth the investment, because classic pieces will have an honored place in your closet and you will enjoy wearing them for a long time. I have some clothes that are more than ten years old and look as elegant today as the day I bought them. The classics never go out of style.

I still have coats that Alex's mother, Diana, gave me. I would sometimes recycle fur coats and have collars and cuffs put on cloth coats or sweaters. She has given me a number of dirndls—lavishly embroidered, lacy folk blouses from Austria and Switzerland—that I have mixed with simple, tailored clothing, and jeans. Those dirndls can go anywhere. They look different—making them chic.

> Simplicity is practically a mantra for me.

As you have probably noticed by now, simplicity is practically a mantra for me. (Less is more.) I love plain white dishes with accent colors, white bed linens with just a touch of color as a border, no clutter anywhere. If you keep it simple, it's hard to go wrong. You can add colorful touches to the basics. My white plates look great with a variety of colorful table linens and fresh flowers, vibrant pillows are scattered on my bed, and I try to have only what we need in our homes, because it makes life so much more manageable, not to mention easier to clean. I'm not a big fan of knickknacks.

In Europe, people prefer well-worn, cherished clothing and seem less concerned about trends. They tend to layer on new looks with their basics whether its jewelry, scarves, a sweater in the color of the season, or the latest jean style. And, of course, a great pair of shoes.

Every well-dressed woman builds her look around a core wardrobe of basic pieces. If you own these pieces, they fit you well, and they are comfortable, you can be ready to go just about anywhere. I think about what I am going to wear while showering. When I am getting ready to go out, I create a storyboard on my bed, laying out different outfits and putting various pieces together. If you see a look that you like in a magazine, try to reproduce it with the clothes you already own. I find Simon Doonan's windows at Barneys an inspiration. Just walking by them gives me a playful sense of what is cutting edge in fashion, and I take those ideas home with me.

WARDROBE ESSENTIALS FOR THE WELL-DRESSED WOMAN

- A pair of great jeans—preferably dark
- A white, long- or three-quarter-sleeved, tailored shirt— Cotton with some spandex for a good fit is the most versatile choice.
- T-shirts—If you want to dress up your look, throw a staple jacket over a tee. It works both ways: If you don't want to look too businesslike or formal, wear a T-shirt under a jacket. Add a statement necklace or a scarf and you're off.
- A pair of black cigarette pants or gray slacks
- A black pencil skirt, or an A-line if more flattering
- A black dress—A sleeveless sheath is elegant. If you don't have the upper arms or body for it, select a style that flows

with sleeves. You could also wear another layer—a jacket or shawl—over the sheath.

- **A wrap dress**—works anywhere—good for most occasions
- **A chic long dress**—for charity events
- **A vest**—I love vests and don't think they are used enough. Whether they are cashmere or wool knits or more tailored, they give a polished, finished look.
- **A blazer**—A blazer is a perfect way to dress up jeans. Cognac is one of my favorite colors.
- **A sweater set in a flattering color has such versatility.** You can dress it up or down with a flirty skirt or jeans.
- **High heels**—Find the highest heels you can that do not cripple you. I prefer a simple pump or slingback. There is no reason to attract too much attention to your feet.
- **Ballet flats**—A pretty pair of flats is great for a casual look.
- **Boots**—I couldn't live without boots. If you take good care of them, they will last forever.
- **A trench coat**—a must
- **An outerwear jacket that's a cross between a biker jacket and a blazer**—this can be worn with a striking scarf at the neck. It's a staple of my wardrobe.
- **A three-quarter-length coat is an option to consider.** It's a flattering length that works well with slacks and skirts—and great with boots. You can go out with it in the evening.
- **A dress coat**—to accommodate longer hemlines
- **A shawl, pashmina scarf, or silk scarf** draped over anything or artfully tied provides an elegant way to add variety.
- **An everyday handbag**—Basic black or an eye-catching color like aubergine. Bags and shoes do not need to match, but they should be in the same family.
- **An evening bag**—I love metallics for night. A clutch that you can tuck under your arm at a party is a great choice.
- **A good watch**—cutting down on the constant need to check your cell phone

$\mathscr{A}$LWAYS OVERDRESS
RATHER THAN UNDERDRESS

Since some people rarely get out of their jeans, and others leave their homes in what looks like their PJs, it's not hard to overdress these days. Rather than showing up at an event looking less than dressed, I believe it's better to risk being overdressed. It feels awful to arrive at a social gathering and find everyone looks great but you, because you haven't put enough effort into how you look. Even if you are wearing jeans, you can top them off with a blouse in a pretty color with a scarf, necklace, jacket, or vest and wear ballet flats, heels, or boots rather than running shoes. You should always try for casual elegance. For this, a blazer is king. You throw it on, and you're dressed.

Overdressing in this context does not mean wearing a business suit to an informal get-together—that would make anyone feel out of place. What I mean is putting effort into how you look and being original. You can jazz up your look with a skirt and a cashmere sweater, an eye-catching necklace, and boots, and you could look and feel smart in a sea of denim and khaki. When in doubt, dress up, not down.

If I'm going to a live performance, I put extra effort into my appearance out of respect for the artists and for other people. You wouldn't believe what people wear to the opera or the theater today. This summer I saw someone in Bermuda shorts and flip-flops at a play. A night at the theater is costly. I am always surprised that people don't want to make the evening a special occasion to get dressed.

I feel the same way about dining out at restaurants and dinner parties—even with close friends. So much goes into preparing a fine meal and entertaining guests. I like to show my appreciation and respect for the effort that went into it for the hostess.

*T*HE COUNTESS'S PANTHEON OF STYLE

- **Chanel**—timeless
- **Givenchy**—legendary; he understood women and elegance
- **Valentino**—timeless and sophisticated
- **Ralph Lauren**—classic, simple look—twin sets, cable knit sweaters
- **Pucci**—I love vintage Pucci—and it travels well.
- **Catherine Malandrino**—for women who are not afraid to express their femininity
- **Galliano at Dior**—takes chances, exciting, chic
- **Ungaro**—classic, elegant, ladylike
- **Yves Saint Laurent**—He liberated women with his pantsuit.
- **Missoni**—wonderful, colorful fabrics that move well and flatter the body; travels well
- **Diane von Fürstenberg**—knows how to make any woman alluring—She invented the wrap dress.

John Galliano and Faycal Amor, my style mentors
(COURTESY OF THE AUTHOR)

Showing up looking as if I made an effort definitely pleases. If you happen to be overdressed, you can always say you've come from another party or are going off to one later.

But you don't need an excuse. Pull out all the stops whenever you like.

𝒯IME FOR THE TREASURE CHEST

If you consider your basics a blank canvas, then your accessories are the paint. Jewelry, scarves, and belts will add flair to your outfits. You should collect accessories, because they help to define personal style. A striking necklace or a belt with a beautiful buckle will add more to your look than a pair of flashy shoes.

Accessories allow you to update your classics. If red is the color of the season, you can pick up touches of red in a scarf or your lipstick. Chandelier earrings might replace pearls for an evening out. A wide or metallic belt might look trendier in certain seasons than a narrow leather one, depending on the look you want to achieve.

It helps if you decide what sort of accessory person you are. I like cocktail rings and big-statement necklaces. But they are not for everyone. Some people collect all sorts of bracelets—but don't stack too many on your arms. It might look great on a supermodel in a photo shoot, but you don't want clanging bracelets to announce your approach. Why is it that I'm always seated next to a woman who wears bangles to the theater?

Pins are fun if you are creative with them. Instead of just plunking a brooch on a lapel, why not do the unexpected and put a flower pin close to your shoulder or a vintage clip on your neckline? You can use a pin to hold a scarf in place or to hold your wrap dress together. You never know when you might need one.

You may be a scarf person. The French are known for their savoir faire when it comes to the scarf. If you don't know what to do with one, flip through fashion magazines for inspiration. A scarf can add a dramatic touch and can accentuate a color that suits you.

And don't forget hair ornaments. My personal favorite is to wear a silk flower, because they never get stale and they add a touch of drama. Even better, a beautiful fresh flower in your hair or tucked behind your ear can be sexy—think Ava Gardner! Using more than an elastic to pull your hair back can give you a polished look—a tortoiseshell clip, a pretty hair claw, an elastic with an ornament, even a small scarf will do the trick.

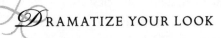

*D*RAMATIZE YOUR LOOK

- A flower in your hair—either fresh or silk
- A fun, flashy cocktail ring—the bigger the better
- A scarf or a shawl around your neck for color and texture
- An eye-catching belt buckle
- A statement pin on your shoulder for the goddess look
- Chandelier earrings or diamond-inspired hoops
- A long strand of pearls worn backward on a dress with a sexy, low-cut back
- Big, fun sunglasses

Make sure you store your accessories so you can look them over quickly to make your selection. A collection of pretty baskets on your dresser is one idea. For belts and necklaces, you can use a hanger designed for the purpose or a tie rack and store them in your closet. If you have room, put hooks to hang things in your closet or on a wall. They can be decorative. All your favorite things will be at eye level.

If your earrings are stored in little boxes or velvet sacks, finding the pair you are looking for can be frustrating. An earring rack can be hung on the back of your closet door or placed on a dresser for your costume jewelry. If you don't have enough drawer space for your scarves, store them in clear plastic bins on a shelf in your closet or under your bed if you are really pressed for space.

Spend time putting together looks so you have less stress when it's curtain time. Accessorizing is a great chance to be creative.

FASHION FAUX PAS

1. **Too much jewelry.** Coco Chanel said always to take one piece off before leaving home. It is better to wear one striking piece of jewelry than several. If you are wearing fabulous earrings, forget the necklace. A special cocktail ring trumps a bracelet. You get the idea—less is more.

2. **Everything matching.** Coordinating your outfit too closely or wearing the same designer head-to-toe is *outré*. Your shoes and purse do not have to match, either, but should be related. I've seen women with matching umbrellas!

3. **Gaudy shoes.** Aside from the height of the heels, I tend to be conservative about shoes. Stay away from shoes in lurid colors or with excessive jeweled ornaments—they can draw too much attention to your feet. You want to create a long silhouette not a show.

4. **Clothing too tight.** Form-fitting clothing is fine, especially if you have a good body, but nothing is more tasteless than looking as if you've been poured into your clothes. Besides, it's terribly uncomfortable and inhibits your movement. I almost wish sizes were hidden so that women would consider fit alone. Don't judge a garment by its size. It's the fit that matters.

5. **Skirt too short.** If you have good legs, you can get away with a higher hem. I say the older you are, the longer the hem should be. Even so, you have to be able to move, bend, and get out of cars without displaying more of you to the world than you would want.

6. **Pale-Leg Syndrome.** If you go bare-legged, think about using a tanning cream. I love Clarins.

7. **Leggings or no leggings.** Unless your legs are well toned and shapely, you should avoid wearing leggings. You can adapt the look by wearing a tunic over leggings to camouflage figure flaws.

8. **Exposing heavy upper arms.** It is better to wear a three-quarter or full sleeve if your upper arms have lost tone. If you must go short-sleeved or sleeveless because you love the dress, a lightweight shawl over your arms looks great.

9. **Sweatpants and sweatshirts.** NEVER! I never wear sweatpants. They are so unflattering. Workout wear has become chic—Juicy Couture is everywhere. There is a great selection of sportswear from the various athletic brands for every figure. If you are full-figured, you will want to wear a long top that covers your hips.

10. **Visible panty lines.** This obvious mistake is easily corrected. If your derrière is in good shape, wear a thong. Don't complain that they're uncomfortable—get used to it. Or try seamless panties with no telltale elastic. Wearing panty hose with a support top or body-shapers like Spanx are an option for those who need slimming. Nothing is worse than panty lines or bulging.

11. **Revealing, low-cut pants.** We live in a low-rise society, so wear low-rise thongs or panties to avoid embarrassing exposure when bending or lifting.

12. **Using a big purse in the evening.** I love big bags, but they stay at home at night. There is no need to lug a daytime bag and all its contents to dinner or during an evening on the town. A small purse is all you need—with a comb, compact, lipstick, tissue, mints, perfume, some dollar bills for restroom tips, fold-up glasses if you need them, and emergency cash for cab fare if necessary.

ℛEAL VS. COSTUME JEWELRY

I am lucky to have a husband who really does have "family jewels." I treasure the de Lesseps' heirloom pieces that my husband and his family have given me. I love the work of the late Andrew Grima, an Italian jeweler who lived in Switzerland. He was once the jeweler of Queen Elizabeth. His work is art—so personalized to you. He made my new wedding ring and many other pieces I treasure.

Yes, I have real jewels locked up in a safe in Switzerland, but I'm wild about costume jewelry. If you don't have the family jewels or Grandma doesn't want to let go of hers just yet, costume jewelry is the answer. Costume jewelry is often more youthful and not as formal as the real thing. It is so well made now that most people can't tell the difference. And there is so much to choose from. From one-of-a-kind designer pieces like Kenny Lane to inexpensive finds in places like Urban Outfitters to handmade work sold on the street, if you develop your eye, you can find jewelry that works anywhere.

> If you wear fake diamonds, you might as well fake it in a big way.

If you wear fake diamonds, you might as well fake it in a big way. Make a statement with your jewelry. Don't be timid. Have fun without trying too hard. I have a fake plastic diamond necklace that looks like a chandelier. It's so over-the-top it's terrific.

Looking for local crafts when you travel can be a great source of jewelry you won't see anyone else wearing at home. I collect Native American jewelry. David Satay's store on Park Avenue always had exceptional pieces, but I found some of my favorites in Canada and the American Southwest.

At a splendid formal event at the Palace Hotel in Gstaad, I wore a diamond necklace that is a de Lesseps heirloom redesigned by Alex's mother, Diana—a work of art. It is a cascade of brilliant diamonds, a showstopper.

One of my friends whispered into my ear, "That's not real, is it?"

Without a moment's hesitation, I touched the necklace and whispered back, "No, of course not."

If you can fool people with the real thing, there is no reason it can't work the other way.

*T*HE THRILL OF THE HUNT

The most fashionable women I know shop at discount stores. They are confident about their taste and know how to judge quality and what works for them. They really don't need a fancy shopping bag—after all, you don't wear the bag! Many designers have their own outlet stores where you can find their clothing discounted significantly. What is on sale may be overstock, meaning more items were manufactured than necessary, or they may be styles that just didn't sell in the stores.

If you have a good eye and a lot of patience, you will enjoy going through the racks at Loehmann's, TJ Maxx, Marshalls, Annie Sez, Daffy's, Century 21, H&M, and other discount stores. These stores offer something for every budget and a wide range of brands. Tucked in between the Willi Smith and BCBG Girls, you can find a beautiful sweater from Italy, an Armani jacket, or a Karl Lagerfeld blouse. And there is a huge selection of affordable, stylish clothing—often a great source of trendy items. But just make sure you do not buy something just because the price is *so good*. Don't talk yourself into buying anything. While shopping, my motto is: *When in doubt, duck.* This is where girlfriends do come in handy. If a dress is right for you, you know it. Trust yourself or a good girlfriend.

> While shopping, my motto is: When in doubt, duck.

I had an impromptu TJ Maxx party once for a couple of my girlfriends on a rainy Saturday in the Hamptons. We brought our kids, who were the same age. We had an hour to put together an outfit with fifty dollars each. It was great to see how far the money went and what fashion geniuses my friends are. We had so much fun modeling our outfits for each other in the dressing room. We did remarkably well and looked as if we had spent a lot more.

*T*aking Inventory

At the end of every season, you should go through your closets and drawers with your most honest and dearest friend and pull out pieces you have not worn. Put them into the maybe pile. Maybe they never fit well or seemed like a good idea at the time. If they are still there the next year, consider getting rid of them. I always pack clothes up and give them away to charity or to someone else who can enjoy them.

Of course, you won't want to toss out classics that you have spent a fortune on and that you may mix with new clothing. Those might have to stay in the maybe pile a little longer.

A Pucci turtleneck might be great with a cashmere cardigan. A vintage tuxedo suit might come in handy someday. A Chanel-inspired suit might be good for an afternoon wedding. If it is classic, fits well, and is comfortable, put it away for a while. You never know when it will seem like just what you need. There is nothing worse than missing something you've given away too quickly. I've learned my lesson.

When you review what you already own, you will know where you need to fill in for the new season, reducing the seductive power of all the new clothes. Having what you already own in mind will help you avoid repeat and impulse buys, leaving room for a few new pieces that complement your existing wardrobe.

STRESS-FREE DRESSING
FOR SPECIAL OCCASIONS

Never buy anything just for one occasion. Nothing is more wasteful than buying a fussy dress that you will never wear again. But if you must, make sure you have an idea of what you want. Impulse shopping happens when you are under pressure, and those mistakes can be costly. Don't feel compelled to buy chiffon, pastels, or patterns.

> Never buy anything just for one occasion.

You should shop your closet, looking for luxurious basics that will always be sophisticated and chic. Those pieces will not date. If you have bought wisely in the past, you will have separates for dressing up that you can mix. Black silk pants or skirt with a lace blouse,

THE PERFECT WEEKEND BAG

When you are going away for the weekend, your travel outfit should consist of the bulkiest items that would take up space in your weekend bag. Wear your blazer and boots or thick soled shoes rather than trying to pack them. Then pack:

- T-shirts/tailored cotton shirt
- Jeans
- Light sweater
- Blazer/leather jacket
- Dress—just in case Givenchy isn't there to dress you if an opportunity arises. Make sure it's one that travels well and that you can accessorize—a solid-color jersey or knit would be perfect.
- Skirt
- Accessories—something easy that mixes with everything
- Ballet flats
- Dress shoes
- Flip-flops/boots (depending on the season)
- PJs that work outside your bedroom, in case the entrance to the bathroom is in the hall
- I keep a set of travel toiletries ready to go.

Packing Tip: Princess Hohenlohe taught me to roll up my dresses when packing and to put the rolled-up garment in a plastic bag. I use plastic grocery bags for this purpose—think green. Pack the plastic bags tightly. The bags keep the clothes from sliding around in your luggage. You just shake them out when you unpack and voilà—no wrinkles.

velvet jacket, or a silk tunic, a perfect black dress with wonderful jewelry, a simple satin dress in a sumptuous color cut on the bias. For daytime events, like weddings or graduations, a pretty suit or simple dress in a jewel tone is perfect. You can add finishing touches to freshen up your look. A witty evening purse, a big bracelet, sparkling earrings, or a magnificent shawl will make your outfit memorable.

It's always worth checking designer sales to find pieces to add to your dressy wardrobe. You can find treasures at sales that might have been beyond your budget otherwise. You don't even have to have an event in mind. If you see something that is perfect for you, works with what you already own, and is in keeping with your lifestyle, don't hesitate.

Time for a quick getaway. Now it's time to tell you more about Honeychile, who was always ready to go.

$\mathscr{P}$ART TWO

The Art of Making
Other People Comfortable

(PHOTO BY MARILI FORASTIERI)

At home

(PHOTO BY MARILI FORASTIERI)

Social Graces

𝒜 CHARMED LIFE

One of the most charming people I've ever known was Princess Hohenlohe, better known as Honeychile. A Georgia peach, she had worked as Bob Hope's sidekick starting at the Palace Theater in New York City and then in movies and on the radio. Their slogan used to be "Where there's Hope there's Honey." She became so famous as a social gadfly in New York that she inspired Truman Capote to create Holly Golightly of *Breakfast at Tiffany's*. Though she was in her seventies when we met, she became my dear friend and mentor.

She married Prince Fritz Alexander Hohenlohe-Waldenburg-Schillingsfürst of Germany. After his death, she made Marbella, Spain, her home but traveled everywhere with great style and energy, welcomed and feted by her countless friends. Honey was a people magnet. She had a way of making a grand entrance. She was lively and open and made people laugh. She was one of those people whom everyone adored—charm personified.

Charm is a way of getting the answer yes
without asking a clear question.
—*Albert Camus*

When we met, my schedule was very free—I only had to tape my TV show in Italy once a week—so we ended up spending a lot of time together. All of Europe was our playground. She took me to her home in Marbella and visited me in Milan. Traveling with her was an extraordinary education. She knew *tout le monde,* everyone who was anyone.

Princess Hohenlohe was welcomed everywhere. She was outrageous—one of those charming eccentrics who was always the life of the party. She made anyone with whom she spoke feel fascinating in the light of her attention. She had a quick wit and a seemingly endless collection of great jokes, which she delivered with enviable style. She told me a lot of those jokes, and they're now part of my repertoire. I can't tell most of them, but here are a couple suitable for publication:

A writer escapes to the Alps to write a book in peace. There is a knock on the door. It's a neighbor inviting him to a party. The neighbor says, "Would you like to come to my party? There's only one little problem. There'll be fighting, gambling, and sex."

The writer says, "It's okay. I'll come, but what should I wear?"

The neighbor says, "It doesn't matter. It's just the two of us."

·

And here's another: "Why don't condoms come in black?"

". . . because they make you look too thin."

·

Being just a little bit naughty often has great appeal.

ℋOW TO MAKE AN ENTRANCE (HONEYCHILE-STYLE)

- Never leave the house without thinking you might be making an entrance. You never know if you're going to run into someone—perhaps a prince.
- Pull yourself together before you enter a restaurant or a party, whatever the size.
- Fix your hair, check your makeup, and smooth out your clothes.
- Pull your shoulders back and enter standing straight and tall. Don't fumble with your purse, adjust your clothes, or look down. Think energy, elegance, and poise.
- Smile and pause for just a moment. Take a deep breath to bring light into your eyes. Let your eyes sweep the room and make eye contact when possible. Chances are someone will come up to greet you. If not, who cares?
- If no one greets you, enter the room in a purposeful way. It's all about vitality. If you are utterly delighted to be there, I assure you that people will take notice.
- In a restaurant, you will be escorted to your table. Nod and smile at anyone you recognize along the way, but don't interrupt unless your seated friend speaks first.
- At a cocktail party or reception, head for someone you know. If you don't see anyone, just approach someone with your hand out and introduce yourself.
- At a smaller gathering, the host or hostess is likely to introduce you to those you do not know. If not, take it upon yourself to be friendly without abruptly interrupting an ongoing conversation.
- Communicating that you are open and lively will attract others to you like bees to honey.

Because of her Southern charm and age, Honey got away with a lot more than most of us could. Watching her made me realize that rules were meant to be broken, but it takes extreme confidence and abundant goodwill to work.

***Honeychile with the
bobblehead of Bob Hope***
(COURTESY OF THE AUTHOR)

Once, when we were in London, the heir to the Gordon's gin dynasty sent his helicopter to take us to his splendid castle in the countryside for a weekend. At the time, private helicopters were extremely rare. At least they were in my world. For Honey, it was another adventure in a charmed life—one that I aspired to.

We spent a lot of time in Gstaad, vacationland for the top of European society. Honey was always at the center of the scene, and I along with her. I found myself meeting titled nobles from all over the world. It didn't take long before greeting a prince or princess appropriately became second nature to me.

Put yourself in a princess's shoes. Can you imagine how hard it must be to have people stiffen up when they meet you, seeing them reviewing in their mind what they are supposed to do? Of course, these aristocrats were accustomed to putting people at ease and to defusing the awkwardness they often face when meeting people.

I was invited to the baptism of the grandson of King Constantine of Greece—Prince William, Diana's son, was the godfather—and I found myself seated next to the king. We were friends at that point and enjoyed each other's company. In fact, I had been his dinner partner at more than one event. I greeted him with a kiss on both cheeks as he stood regally. Then his sister, Sofia, Queen of Spain, approached, and I became flustered. I hadn't met the queen before, and I didn't know whether to curtsy, genuflect, bow, or kiss her ring.

The truth is that you do not have to observe traditional protocol if you are not a subject of that king or queen—a citizen of the monarch's country. A woman does not have to curtsy or a man bow before someone else's king or queen. But if the event presents itself, why not do the right thing?

𝒥F YOU MEET A KING OR QUEEN

- Women perform a small curtsy (not an extravagant, full court curtsy), men bow from the neck. This is not compulsory.
- If a king or queen extends a hand, do not give it a full handshake. Just touch it briefly.
- The form of address is Your Majesty, followed by ma'am or sir in conversation.
- Never wear gloves in the presence of a king or queen.
- Never continue to eat if a king or queen has stopped.
- Do not kiss the royal hand, put your arm around the king or queen, or turn your back on royalty.

In speech, except for extremely formal occasions, all ranks below duke are called lord and lady. For example, the Earl and Countess of Perrin are called Lord and Lady Perrin.

So unless you know or someone tells you, it might be hard to make the distinction among various ranks. Honey always coached me beforehand.

*H*OW TO ADDRESS AN ARISTOCRAT
(IN THE ORDER OF THEIR IMPORTANCE)

Title	Addressed in speech
King/Queen	Your Majesty or Your Royal Majesty the first time in conversation, followed by sir/madam or ma'am
Princes, Princesses, Members of the Royal Family	Your Royal Highness, followed by sir/ma'am
Duke/Duchess	Your Grace (by social inferiors) Duke/Duchess (by social equals) the first time in conversation, followed by sir/madam or ma'am
Marquess (Duke's eldest son) /Marchioness	Lord/Lady Devonshire (the name of the region or castle)—the first time in conversation, followed by my lord/my lady
Duke's Daughter	Lady (first name)
Earl (the eldest son of Marquess or Count)/Countess (Earl's or Count's wife)	Lord (title)/Lady (name of region or castle), Count or Countess followed by sir/ma'am
Viscount (Earl's eldest son)/ Viscountess **Do not pronounce s**	Lord (region)/ Lady (region or first name)
Baron/Baroness	Lord (region)/Lady (region)
Knight or Baronet / Wife of Knight or Baronet	Sir (first name)/Lady (first name), followed by sir/ma'am

$\mathscr{S}$OCIAL GRACE AS AN ACQUIRED SKILL

Not too long ago, learning manners, poise, and tact was a fundamental part of everyone's education. People aspired to be sophisticated and soigné. Think of celebrity icons—debonair men like Fred Astaire, Cary Grant, even Frank Sinatra, or confident, polished women like Ingrid Bergman, Greta Garbo, Grace Kelly, Katharine Hepburn, Catherine Deneuve. But the world has changed. Casual Fridays mean more than just a relaxation of dress codes in our society. People have lost sight of the fact that some rules make life easier. "Anything goes" has resulted in an abundance of unattractive, selfish behavior that assaults our senses. The wince factor is getting higher every day.

The fact is that personal contact has been reduced in our culture. In the office, e-mail has replaced phone calls. ATMs have replaced bank tellers, and we pump our own gas and pay with a credit card. There are drive-through coffee shops, banks, dry cleaners, even liquor stores. We shop at big stores with very little service. We even check ourselves out at the supermarket. Kids would prefer to text-message than talk on their cell phones. It all seems extremely impersonal.

When the need for everyday courtesy is minimized, many people are left baffled and unsure of how to behave in more demanding social situations. Clearly, people aren't learning about social graces in school or at home. After watching *The Real Housewives of New York City,* people of all ages write to me expressing their insecurity and their desire to know the ground rules. And that's just what I aim to provide in this section of *Class with the Countess.*

Social graces help to smooth the way in our relationships with others. Knowing what to do or say at the appropriate time will reduce your social anxiety. If you are confident about how to behave, you are free to be concerned about others. The key to social grace is consideration and respect for other people. The good news is that it's all based on common sense. If you can stop being self-conscious and think about how others feel instead, you will be able to act with natural grace. Once you are no longer nervous and timid about how to act in various social situations, you will be able to approach others with true warmth and friendliness. So stop worrying about being "proper." Being considerate of others is at the heart of charm and grace.

> Being considerate of others is at the heart of charm and grace.

MAKING INTRODUCTIONS

Making introductions is a fundamental social skill. An introduction is an important moment. This exchange is a critical point in social interaction when sometimes indelible first impressions are made. Depending on your role, it's your chance either to smooth the way for two people who are unacquainted or to charm someone new. When you make an introduction, look at the person to whom you are making the introduction, then turn to the person you are presenting as you finish. It is always good to give a line or two about what the people have in common as a jumping-off point for conversation.

Determining who gets priority in an introduction—that is, who get introduced to whom—is easy, because the rules are clear-cut:

Introducing People to Someone in Authority
"Mr. Benson, I would like you to meet our new intern, Dan Heller. He is in his senior year at USC."

"Dan, this is our CEO, Mr. Benson."

In this instance, Dan should smile and wait for Mr. Benson to extend his hand.

Introducing Men to Women
"Alexis, I'd like you to meet Jerome Kerner. He's a great tennis player, and I know how much you enjoy the sport."

"Jerome, this is Alexis Johnson, who just won the town's women's singles event."

Generally, a woman should extend her hand first. Always with a smile.

Introducing Younger People to Older People
"Mother, I'd like you to meet Barbara, my friend from Paris."

"Barbara, I'm so glad to be introducing you to my mother at last."

In this case, the older person extends her hand first.

Introducing a Single Person to a Group
Here you should address the group first, to get everyone's attention.

"Tom, Joan, and Steve, I'd like you to meet Ronnie Reeves, who just moved to town."

"Ronnie, this is Tom Harriot, Joan Miller, and Steve Wong."

Ronnie should shake Joan's hand first.

Introducing Yourself
At a party, you will often have to take it upon yourself to introduce yourself to other guests. Do so with a warm smile.

"Hello, I'm Patricia Stone. Nice to meet you."

A WORD ON HANDSHAKES

It used to be that a man would never extend his hand unless a woman extended hers first.

That rule has relaxed somewhat, maybe because so many women are in business. Now the highest ranking or the oldest often makes the first move. You will have to be observant here. If no one extends a hand, don't hesitate, especially if you are a woman.

If you are introduced to a group of people, shake the hand of the woman first.

When You Are Introduced

Always smile and pay close attention to the name and use it in your response. "It's a pleasure to meet you, Anne Marie." Even though these are informal times, you should address anyone who has a position of authority or is older than you as Mr., Mrs., Dr., until they ask you to call them by their first names. When people seem tongue-tied about how to address me because of my title, I'll say, "Please call me LuAnn" or "Please call me Mrs. de Lesseps." You know how you want to be addressed. It's up to you to state the preference. You should also remember to use the names by which people are introduced. I always make a rhyme in my mind to help. Charles should not become Charlie, and Victoria should not become Vicky.

If you didn't hear or don't remember the name of the person you are meeting, just ask. "I'm sorry, I missed your last name" or "Would you please tell me your name again?" This can help you avoid embarrassment later when you have to introduce this person to someone else.

If you are sitting, stand when a person is being introduced to you. Women can remain seated, but most do stand today. I think everybody should stand, unless you're attached to an IV.

When Someone Neglects to Introduce You

Sometimes you might join two people who are talking, because you know one of them. If that person forgets to introduce you after you greet him, wait for a pause in the conversation and introduce yourself to the person you don't know. Simply say, "Hello, I'm Sophie." Chances are the person you know has assumed you already know the other person or has forgotten your name. It is easy to smooth over what could be an awkward situation or one that would make you feel ignored. Don't assume the worst. I never do.

Introduction Gaffes

It happens to all of us. We draw a blank on someone's name. Sometimes if you pause, the person you are introducing will be astute enough to see your hesitation for what it is and jump right in and introduce herself. I wait until the last possible moment just in case. If that doesn't work, it's best just to be out with it—"I'm sorry, I'm terrible with names, and I've forgotten yours." Or "Jim, I apologize, but I don't know your last name."

If you are concerned that you will not be able to pronounce someone's name, it's better to say so. "This is Brianne—how did you pronounce your name? You say it so much better than I do." If someone mispronounces your name, it is fine to correct the pronunciation with a smile and a comment: "I know it's hard to pronounce."

Sometimes, as a hostess you know you will be introducing a guest—perhaps a foreign dignitary or an exchange student—whose name you do not know how to pronounce. Find out beforehand and practice. People will be impressed and grateful for your forethought.

Maybe a friend has gotten divorced and gone back to using her maiden name, and you introduce her by her married name, or you get a title wrong. The best thing to do is apologize quickly when you are corrected. Keep it light. Humor goes a long way to taking the embarrassment from such situations. The same goes for the person whose name has been forgotten or mispronounced. Just make the correction with no muss or fuss. The important thing is not to make an issue of a mistake that all of us have made and will undoubtedly make in the future. Don't panic or fixate. Just get over it and move on.

> An elegant person always acts with kindness.

THE AIR KISS

Today, kissing between women or between a man and a woman seems to have replaced a handshake after the initial meeting. The air kiss developed because women don't want to leave a lipstick smudge on someone's cheek. When two women are greeting each other, the older woman should make the first move. A man should wait to see if a woman offers her hand or cheek.

In business, a handshake is preferable, unless you know the person very well.

An elegant person always acts with kindness. When someone makes a social mistake—a quick word or gesture of reassurance, self-deprecating humor, and compassion will help him to save face. Always come to the rescue of someone who has blundered. That person will never forget you for it.

THE INTERNATIONAL AIR KISS

- The Germans and the British tend to be reserved in their greetings. Always offer your hand. It's easy enough to shake hands and lean in for a kiss if a warmer greeting is expected.
- The Italians prefer a handshake or a hug. They always kiss women.
- In the United States, one kiss seems to be the standard.
- The French start with at least two kisses. They begin on the left cheek.
- The Swiss kiss three times, starting on the left.
- The Spanish are effusive with kisses and hugs.
- Asians prefer not to touch and make a quick bow instead. Business people now are comfortable with a handshake.
- For greetings, Arabs will kiss only a person of the same sex.

𝓔VERYDAY MANNERS AND SMALL COURTESIES

Once we've gone past "please," "thank you," "you're welcome," and "excuse me," everyday courtesies seem to be unraveling in our informal time. These gestures are the outward sign of consideration and civility. They make all the difference in the world we live in today. They are usually observed in business, when everyone is on his or her best behavior, but fewer and fewer people extend these courtesies to the people they care about the most or to strangers.

𝓣RADITIONAL GALLANT COURTESIES

- Men are supposed to walk on the street side—originally to protect a woman from splatter from the horses and carriages on the streets. I like that position in New York, because it keeps me closer to the shop windows. It seems this tradition is outdated, but more formal people still observe it.
- A man should offer his arm as he walks down the street with a woman.
- Men should open doors for women.
- Men should open car doors and help women in and out of cars.
- A man should enter a revolving door first to get it going.
- A man should walk before a woman down a steep incline, on uneven ground, or through crowds.
- Men should help women take off and put on their coats.
- A man should offer to help a woman when she is carrying a heavy bag or many packages.

I still love the traditional courtesies men offer women, and I think the world would be a more pleasant place—or at least a more flirtatious one—if everyone observed them. I think men should rise when a woman enters a room. If I excuse myself from a table, I expect the gesture that the men are about to get up, but I always say, "Please, don't get up." Same when I return.

It's not that I can't open a door myself, need a man's support to walk down the street, can't manage a slope, or don't have the strength to push a revolving door or to get out of a car on my own steam. I like what these gestures symbolize. They're signs of respect and appreciation. There is something sweet about the notion that they are caring for me,

Why not be put on a pedestal?

that I need to be protected in this way. Why not be put on a pedestal? These gestures give you a chance to show your appreciation by saying thank you.

Of course, a woman can reciprocate or treat others the same way. If you see anyone struggling with a coat, give a hand. A photographer recently came to my home to take some shots for a home style magazine. Upon leaving, he asked for his coat. Much to his surprise, I helped him on with it. He was clearly pleased.

Likewise, if you see someone carrying many packages, you should offer assistance. If you see an elderly person behind you, open the door and let that person go through first. When you go through a door, hold it for the person who is following you. Always knock on a closed door—you never know what's happening behind it. Let those inside a building leave before you enter. All of these actions show consideration for others, which is what social grace is all about and what seems to be forgotten.

It's a pity that we can't expect this kind of courtesy from

one another, but you can always try to shape the behavior of others. If you stop briefly at a door, a man will probably take the hint and reach around you to open it. If you turn with a smile and hand him your coat, he will have to help you on with it. There are other cues. You can ask him to drive the car, move something heavy, or help you get something down from the top shelf. Men essentially want to please you. If you thank a man for these gestures and are genuinely pleased by what he has done, I guarantee he will continue with these courtesies. Men want to be acknowledged and appreciated, and that's easy to do when they treat you with courtesy.

Manners on the Move

When you are out and about, everything you do affects those around you. In a crowded, busy city like New York, civility and mindfulness are essential to living harmoniously with such a diverse assortment of people.

On the Sidewalk

- Walk on the right side. Why don't people understand there are two lanes? Groups should not walk abreast, blocking the sidewalk. I wish signs would be posted to that effect.
- If you want to get by someone, pick up your speed and get into the left-lane passing zone. Don't jostle or whack him with what you are carrying as you pass—although it might be tempting in some circumstances.
- Don't stop abruptly. You have no warning brake lights.
- Try to keep pace with everyone else. Pull over if you have to make a call.

- If you run into someone you know, stand aside. You don't want to be in the way of New Yorkers in a hurry.

In Taxis

- Don't push your way in front of someone who has been waiting to hail a cab. Either wait your turn until after that person has found a cab or cross the street.
- Start with hello—most people don't—and give the driver the address. If you want to make him laugh, ask him to take you to Switzerland. If you prefer going a certain way, tell him the route at the start. With certain New York cabbies, it may lead to a debate. You'll have to judge the driver's experience.
- Feel free to ask the driver to turn down the music or to lower his voice while he is arguing with his wife on the phone.
- If you plan to pay by cash, remember drivers rarely take a bill over twenty dollars.
- Some people round up when they tip. If you want to do the right thing, tip 15 to 20 percent if the ride was satisfactory.
- You like to get into a clean cab, so don't leave an empty coffee cup, water bottle, or newspaper behind.

*T*ECH ETIQUETTE

How many wireless devices do you wear? Gone are the good old days when people actually had to talk to one another. Just sit at any Apple store and watch. People become so caught up in their own bubbles that they forget the world around them.

So many of my pet peeves involve electronic devices that are supposed to make communication easy. What people talk about in public on their cell phones amazes me.

I can walk down the street and be treated to arguments, foul language, business deals, and very personal conversations. And how about those annoying novelty ringtones that go off anytime, anyplace?

People slow down to text-message or to read their messages while walking or crossing the street, not paying attention to what's happening around them. Sometimes I fear for their lives! Haven't you been startled by an outburst from someone standing next to you? You might think he's having a psychotic episode, babbling to himself, until you realize he's just talking on a Bluetooth. God, I miss phone booths!

There are several cardinal sins that should be avoided at all costs:

- ❧ **Putting your phone on the table when you arrive at a restaurant.** All electronic devices belong out of sight. You can check to see who has called, but don't pick it up unless it's an emergency.
- ❧ **Disruptive ringing.** Your phone should be turned off in quiet places and meetings—switch to vibrate.
- ❧ **Giving precedence to calls rather than the people you're with.** Taking calls when you are with friends, family, or colleagues is rude. If you are expecting an important call, apologize and inform those you are with before checking your phone to see who is calling. I always answer if one of my children calls or if my husband is calling from his travels—they are top priority. It's the main reason I carry a cell phone.

- ❧ **Serial calls in public places.** Making long calls or one call after another on public transportation or in public places is inconsiderate. Some people think the world is their office.
- ❧ **Making calls in elevators.** Texting works best.
- ❧ **Talking too loudly or offensively.** Why should anyone have to be exposed to unwelcome glimpses of another person's life? It is like secondhand smoke. You just can't escape it.
- ❧ **Holding a phone or text-messaging while driving.** It is tempting, but against the law in many states, not to use an earphone so that both your hands are free for driving. Taking your eyes off the road to dial, read, or send a message is just plain dangerous.
- ❧ **Not being able to resist glancing at your e-mails at a meeting or restaurant.** Few things are more irritating than speaking to someone who is obviously distracted. I feel as if I'm wasting my time, because someone else's time is more important.
- ❧ **Writing e-mails that never end.** Keep your messages brief, especially since so many people are reading their messages on handheld devices. And only pass on the best of jokes and articles you receive from friends. We're all being inundated. I still prefer a good old-fashioned phone call.

> I still prefer a good old-fashioned phone call.

A business e-mail should be returned in a day or two, a social e-mail within a week unless it's an RSVP, which you should respond to promptly. By the way, refrain from making your e-mails high priority unless it's justified. It's annoying when routine correspondence automatically requires acknowledgment of receipt. Use that option for important matters only or if you are having a hard time reaching someone. You know who you are.

Another of my pet peeves is listening to epic messages left on my voice mail. Don't be long-winded after the beep. Leave a brief message and your number. Make certain you say your number slowly and clearly. It's a good idea to give your number after you initially identify yourself and again at the end of the message. That way, the person you are calling does not have to listen to the whole message again to get your number.

A WORD ON CALL WAITING

All of us like the notion of people not getting a busy signal when we are on the phone, but it's worth having the call bounce to your voice mail rather than interrupting a conversation. If you are expecting an important call, it is fine to excuse yourself for a moment or to ask the person to whom you are talking if you can call back. I think it's rude to keep someone waiting too long while you answer the other call.

RESTAURANT ETIQUETTE

I love dining out. Let's face it: It's a treat to be served and not have to cook or clean up. Instead, you get to think about what you're going to wear to be dazzling. I love all foods, but I must say Mediterranean cuisine is my favorite. I have wonderful memories of one restaurant in Italy, which was like a dollhouse. There must have been five tables or six at the most. The menu had three dishes from which to choose, prepared by the mamas of the neighborhood.

*R*ESTAURANT FAUX PAS

1. Taking your coat, umbrellas, shopping bags, and briefcases to the table. It's best not to clutter—check them when you enter.
2. Talking or laughing loudly. Be subdued. You don't want to disturb others, and you certainly don't want people to eavesdrop. You never know who is listening.
3. Putting your purse, briefcase, or phone on the table. Your purse belongs on your lap or the floor. Hanging your handbag on the back of your chair is not a good idea, but I always do it. A word to the wise: Pickpockets have been known to operate in good restaurants.
4. Calling out or snapping your fingers to get the attention of your server. If a quiet "excuse me" or a subtle gesture doesn't work, ask a busboy or the maître d' to send your waiter over.
5. Talking on your cell phone or sending e-mails. Don't— not in the company of others. If you are expecting an important call, have your phone on vibrate and excuse yourself from the table.
6. Picking up anything you drop. Just get the attention of a waiter or busboy and ask him for a replacement fork or whatever has fallen. At fine restaurants, someone will be there to help you before you can ask.
7. Brushing crumbs or stacking plates. That's what the waitstaff is for.

The most elegant restaurants make you feel as if you are eating in a private home. And they don't have to be fancy. Four-star restaurants deliver service fit for a king, but many fine restaurants are like having a warm family meal. Both are great dining experiences.

It's always a good idea to call for a reservation if the restaurant is in a city or if you are dining with a party of six or more or trying a popular restaurant. At certain restaurants in New York, getting a table can sometimes take contacts. Use your connections if you have any. If you are running late, call the restaurant to let them know. It's only courteous, and you certainly don't want them to give your table away. Don't expect to get the table you asked for if you are late.

If You're Seated in Siberia

In New York and most cities, people want to see and be seen. They want a front row seat for celebrity sightings and a good view of the overall scene.

If you find yourself being led to a table by the restrooms, the kitchen, too close to a workstation, or too near a colleague, politely ask the maître d' or the hostess if another table is available. If possible, they will accommodate you. When you make the reservation, ask for a table in a location you want—on the terrace, in the front room or the back, upstairs or down, perhaps a booth. I prefer tables near the wall and not in the middle of the room. If you're desperately unhappy, leave.

Once you have looked at the menu, heard the specials, and decided what you want to eat, close the menu and put it down in front of you. That signals to your waiter that you are ready to order. If you haven't decided, let others go first. This way, you know whether or not to order a first course.

Usually, everyone at the table orders the same number of courses. No one likes to eat alone or to watch someone else eat. If you weren't planning to order a first course or a dessert and everyone else does, you can always order a simple salad, or biscotti or berries for the table.

TASTING THE WINE

The little ritual when a sommelier or wine steward opens a bottle of wine has a simple purpose—to determine that the wine is not corked, meaning it has not spoiled during shipping or storage.

In the best restaurants in France, the sommelier will taste the wine. In the United States, the sommelier will pour a little of the wine for the diner to taste. If you're the taster, hold the glass by the stem and swirl the wine a bit. This releases the bouquet. Put your nose at the mouth of the glass and smell. Think cork in order to tell if the wine is good. If you smell cork, it's off. Ask for another bottle.

Take a sip. You do not have to comment on or critique the wine. All you have to say is, "That's fine." If you have asked the sommelier to suggest the wine, you can say, "Excellent choice" or "Very nice" if you don't have the wine vocabulary down.

Sending Food Back

My father-in-law, Victor Comte de Lesseps, the ambassador, sent food back to the kitchen all the time, to our great embarrassment. He was demanding and knew exactly what he preferred. The waiters, who tried nervously to please such an eminent person, really had to be on their toes. One time at the Amstel in the Hague, he ordered a fish, and it was brought to him filleted. He exploded. "I ordered a fish with a head and a tail. I want the whole fish." He wasn't a fan of nouvelle cuisine and liked to filet his own fish.

Regardless of what has happened, be polite and discreet about the problem. Never be overbearing or indignant. Do not become angry with your server. Chances are it was not his fault. If the wrong dish is served to you or you find a foreign object in your food, don't hesitate to send the dish back. If it is a question of preparation and the dish is not that off, you might decide to keep it. Returning it could be more trouble than it's worth. The person or people you are eating with might feel obligated to wait for you to be served, though if their food is hot, they should not wait. If they start their meal, you'll have some catching up to do, which could be uncomfortable for everyone. It's your choice.

Paying the Bill

There is nothing worse than the tension of bill time. It's annoying when people divvy up the bill. There is so much confusion leading to an unattractive situation. In the best and choicest of all possible worlds, one person treats. Many friends just take turns treating one another. If you are planning to pick up the tab, you can make arrangements when you call for a reservation or speak with the maître d' when you arrive. You can sign for the meal then, so that no transactions take place at the table. That way, you avoid the "let me take care of this" reach for the bill and the tug-of-war that might ensue. Whether you are going on a date or are with friends, it's better to be clear about who is paying going into the meal.

Another option is to divide the bill equally, which tends to even out if you see these friends regularly. If you are on a tight budget and have to order carefully, you might say so in advance when the restaurant is initially chosen. That way, you can avoid going to a place that is beyond your means. Ordering the omelet while your friends eat filet mignon and expect you to share equally can be stressful. If you don't manage the situation beforehand by suggesting a restaurant that is affordable, you will just have to bite the bullet and toss your credit card in with the others.

Some friends might be sensitive to the situation and will say, "You've eaten so little—your share should be less." That person might discreetly give you the difference in cash. This is fine, but you definitely want to avoid complicated calculations, the exchange of money, including piles of coins, at the table.

The Count and the Doggie Bag

My father-in-law was visiting us in the Hamptons. I took him to the Palm; we ordered a five-pound lobster, which we barely made a dent in. I asked our waiter to pack it up so we could take it home. The count was appalled. He'd never heard of a doggie bag. Taking leftovers from a restaurant seemed utterly disgusting to him.

The next day, I made a delicious pasta with the leftover lobster. He couldn't believe that his meal from the previous evening had been reinvented as lunch. He saw the point of not wasting the food and realized that portions are usually so small in Europe that there is never anything left to take away. If he could become a convert, you shouldn't hesitate or be shy to take home what you cannot finish.

TIPPING

Valet parking—$2 to $3 at pickup or $1 to $2 on each end.

Maître d'—usually is not tipped. If you have requested a special table or if you are a large party, you should tip him $10.

Coat check—$1 per item

Waiter—15 or 20 percent of the bill before taxes

Bartender—$1 per drink

Restroom attendant—$1

TRAVEL ETIQUETTE

I just wish I didn't have to take off my shoes—eew! It has become a nightmare to travel, breeding anxiety, impatience, and selfishness. Traveling can be grueling, because there are so many long lines and rules and regulations, and let's face it, the security people often aren't nice. If you feel yourself getting short-tempered and ready to rumble, think about your destination. That's the only thing that keeps me going—getting there.

Alex and I travel all the time, so we're organized and ready to go. I have a little red case packed with travel-size toiletries that I just pop into my carry-on bag. Knowing the rules of what you can carry onto the plane before you go will spare your halting the line at security as the guard goes through your carry-on and confiscates your special hand lotion or perfume. Not only do you lose a significant beauty product, you also have to deal with the irritation of the people behind you on line.

THE FRIENDLY SKIES

- Wear socks. Walking barefoot through security is horrid.
- Make sure every bag you are checking has an identification tag before you get to the airport. Take off the old airport tags so your bag doesn't end up on your last trip.
- Do take off your belt for security. It's not worth being frisked.
- If there are delays or a cancellation, be kind to your counter agent or you might never get bumped into business.
- Rushing ahead only delays the boarding process. You'll be on the plane long enough.
- Avoid letting your carry-on hit people who are seated on the aisles as you find your seat. Carry those bags in front of you.
- While reaching for the overhead bin, be careful about mooning other passengers.
- Let the person behind you know when you are going to recline your seat. I love it when people tell me.
- Don't grab the seat in front of you to stand up, or slap your tray table up.
- Silicone earplugs are a must.
- Since they no longer feed you, bring your own meal. Be sure to avoid food with strong odors.
- Don't be rude to the flight attendants, but don't accept being bullied either. You are the client, after all.
- Don't spill over to another seat or the aisle. Planes are tight. People have a right to be territorial—especially on a long flight.
- Don't carry on loud conversations no matter how much alcohol you have consumed.
- If you're lucky enough to find somebody you want to talk to, stand in the galley instead of the aisle.
- Don't stay in the restroom too long to do a complete makeover before landing.

My husband is a stickler for arriving early, because you never know. You might get stuck in traffic, and the check-in and security lines can be long. Blah, blah, blah. Though it seems to me that we sit at the airport forever waiting for our flight, I've come to agree that it's better to be at the airport ready to go than stressing about making our flight. As others melt down around you, you can take it all in stride.

How to Stop a Chatterbox

If you find yourself next to a compulsive talker who is about to launch into his life story or is asking you about yours, it is not difficult to end the conversation. After a few pleasantries, you can answer questions with a simple yes or no. Your seatmate should get the idea. If you want to avoid the situation completely, use your earphones or immediately pull out a book, magazine, or laptop. I've met some of the most interesting people I know on planes—but it's rare.

When Your Seatmate Is Sleeping, Check His Breathing

The worst sort of spillover is when your neighbor falls asleep and leans on you, his head falls on your shoulder, or he is a noisy sleeper. Say "excuse me" or tap him lightly to get him to move or quiet down. If you have to leave your seat, do the same thing, then apologize for waking him.

Alex's brother, Ferdinand, a race-car driver who won the world championship in 1992 in LeMans and Daytona, was on a flight to race in Japan. He was seated next to a man whose head kept falling on Ferdinand's shoulder. Ferdinand would gently push the man away each time. He was exasperated when the man leaned heavily against him. Then he realized, to his horror, that his seatmate was dead. Now, as a nurse, I've come to people's rescue during flights, but I've never had anyone die on me!

When in Beijing

Alex and I once got lost on a walk in Beijing. Whenever we walked to a hotel we thought was ours, it wasn't. It was starting to get dark. We didn't speak a word of Chinese, and we could not find a single person on the streets who could speak English—even the cabbies didn't recognize "Palace Hotel." We couldn't read any of the signs. Then I remembered I had a card from the hotel in my back pocket. All we had to do was flash it to a cabbie, and we were on our way.

Always carry a card from your hotel with you when you are out and about, especially if you don't speak the language.

If you are traveling to a foreign country, you will want to learn about the country before you arrive there, either by reading a guidebook or checking online resources. You should familiarize yourself with customs that are different from ours. Respect pays a big part in how you are received by the people whose country you are visiting. Dress codes vary greatly from country to country, and what may be perfectly acceptable here might

> **Always carry a card from your hotel with you when you are out and about, especially if you don't speak the language.**

be considered immodest elsewhere. It's important to learn the most basic of conversational phrases. Being able to say "hello," "good-bye," "thank you," and "excuse me" will go a long way to receiving a warm welcome.

It will also save you a lot of fumbling if you learn the currency. The euro, the only currency used by the European Union, has made it a lot easier than converting lira, francs, drachmas, and as many currencies as there are countries.

A WORD ON JET LAG

On long flights, eat a meal before boarding—you won't be missing much—or right when you take your seat. Digestion sets your body's clock. It's best not to drink alcohol, because it disrupts your sleep and dehydrates you—and I like to sleep on long trips. But if you are a nervous flyer and a drink helps you relax, go for it. This is where sleeping pills are a must.

A Travel Nightmare

Alex and I were traveling with a group of friends in Myanmar and my father had joined us. He'd never been to Asia, and I wanted to share this once-in-a-lifetime experience with him. My father and I decided to go back to Switzerland a little early, because I missed the children. Alex made all the arrangements, and we left the group early. As we drove to the airport, I spotted a roadside market with women selling Burmese crafts and treasures. It was irresistible. I asked the driver to pull over so that I could pick up some last-minute gifts.

After buying a few Christmas presents, we again headed to

the airport. When we started to go through Passport Control, I reached into my purse and my father's passport was not where I thought it was. The panic set in. My mother's words rang in my ears, "Take good care of your father." I didn't know what had happened to his passport. We had traveled to so many different places in the country, it could have been anywhere. So there we were—our driver had left and no one spoke English. A card from the hotel came to the rescue again. We called the hotel and they were able to send the car back. Thank God for miracles!

As my father and I tried to figure out where we lost the passport, we realized simultaneously that it might have fallen out of my purse at the market. We had to backtrack. We pulled over when we reached the market, and a Burmese woman came running to the car, waving my father's passport over her head. We were so relieved, but we had missed our flight. I knew I was in major trouble with Alex after he had rearranged everything for our early departure. Shopping at a roadside market would never be an acceptable excuse for ruining the plans he had made especially for us. I asked my father to tell a little white lie—that we had dropped the passport in the lobby or left it at the desk. If Alex knew the truth about my last-minute impulse buying, he would lose it. So when you're on your way back to an airport in a third-world country, don't get out of the car to shop. I didn't tell Alex the truth until two years later. He laughed, but he wouldn't have enjoyed the story then.

(PHOTO BY MARILI FORASTIERI)

The Art of Conversation

*I*T'S NOT ONLY ABOUT BEING DAZZLING

Some of the best conversations happen naturally. It's a magical meeting of the minds or spirit. But if it isn't effortless, sometimes it's better to say nothing than to say the wrong thing. A lot of people talk too much rather than being in the moment. It's an anxious response—as if they can't allow a pause and have to fill in the space. You can always tell when someone is struggling in conversation, because it feels uncomfortable. In the end, it's not what you say but how you say it and how it's delivered.

My experience is that a sense of humor and not taking yourself too seriously helps break down barriers. Being able to talk to anybody about anything is one of the prerequisites of elegance. The art of conversation is a balancing act that involves when to listen and when to speak, when to respond and when to initiate. If you feel at all out of your element, it is better to say less and look interested. That way you are not likely to say anything silly and set yourself up for social failure.

ℳN OPENING LINE THAT OPENED THE DOOR

Never underestimate the value of a good opening line. I was sitting at a café in Rome with a friend when a man came up to me and asked if I knew who Sharon Stone was. I'd heard of her, but *Basic Instinct* hadn't yet opened in Rome. He told me that he needed someone to play Sharon Stone and asked me if I could do it. At first, I thought, "He's putting me on," but then I realized he was serious.

He explained that they wanted me to play Sharon Stone on the equivalent of the Emmys in Italy. She was supposed to be presenting an award, and they were planning a buffo joke for the show. That is how I found myself backstage at the biggest awards show in Italy, wearing a blond wig and pretending to be Sharon Stone. As I was waiting backstage to make my appearance as Sharon, MacGyver (Richard Dean Anderson), was having his makeup done—*MacGyver* was one of the most popular shows in Italy at the time.

MacGyver said to me, "Didn't we meet at a party in L.A.?"

And I said, "Yes, of course," realizing he didn't know I wasn't Sharon Stone.

Arnold Schwarzenegger, who costarred with Sharon Stone in one of her first films, nudged me and said, "Play the part."

I was terrified to get on the stage with Elton John, Ramazzotti (an Italian singer star), Melanie Griffith, and Pavarotti in the audience.

As I got ready to walk out on the stage, Silvio Berlusconi, the prime minister of Italy and the owner of Fininvest, a media and finance company, came backstage to say hello to the workers. Berlusconi owned three TV channels, and Fininvest was one of the ten largest privately owned companies in Italy. Imagine if Rupert Murdoch were president—that is how powerful Berlusconi is. The entire backstage crew was silent, waiting for him to acknowledge them or shake their hands.

I had to walk by Mr. Berlusconi to get onstage. As I passed, my opening line was "How nice it must be to have the whole world stop when you walk by."

He looked at me, bowed with a sweeping gesture, and said, "After you."

I sashayed in my gown and wig onto the elaborate stage. I didn't look a thing like Sharon Stone, but who knew, except for Arnold Schwarzenegger?

The host interviewed me briefly. "So, Sharon," he asked me, "how was it to work with Michael Douglas?" I had to answer in broken, elementary Italian as we chatted. My Italian was less than perfect at the time. Then the host said, "The award goes to . . ."

A girl came out with the award, which I took. "Oh, thank you so much. This means so much to me." As I gushed over the award, the people who actually won it were heading for the stage.

"Sharon, this award really isn't for you," the host said as he reached for the statue.

"What?? Noooo!" I proceeded to have a fit on the stage. "I came all the way from L.A. I thought I was getting an award for *Basic Instinct*. You can't give this award to them." I clutched it to my breast.

The winners, who were in on the joke, tried to take the award from me. There was pandemonium onstage. During the mayhem, I glanced at the audience and saw Arnold Schwarzenegger looking around and I said, "Ciao, Arnie," and blew him a kiss. The camera panned the audience, and there was Berlosconi with a huge grin on his face.

The whole prank went off very well. I was far from an actress, but I threw myself into it and made it work. I went to the after-party thinking, "Oh, well, that's what it's like to be a star."

At the party, Berlusconi approached me. He asked, "Who *are* you and why aren't you working for me?"

"I do work for you," I responded, "but I'm always the girl behind the star."

"Not anymore" was the prime minister's instant response.

I couldn't believe it. I was at the right place at the right time. But it was my opening line that initially got Prime Minister Berlusconi's attention. Three months later, Berlusconi called my agent, offering me a job as a cohost of the popular Italian soccer show called *Pressing*.

BREAKING THE ICE

There is never a reason to stand alone at a cocktail party or large reception. Just go up to someone and introduce yourself. Chances are that person will be relieved by your attention. The good news is that starting a conversation gets easier the more often you do it. Your mission is to uncover something interesting about that other person. The idea is to elicit a response that will be the start of a conversation that might give you an idea of what interests the other person. This works even for the painfully shy.

Whatever you do, don't start a conversation by asking, "What do you do?" That's a dead giveaway that you have nothing else to talk about other than work. That information might well come out in the course of a conversation.

---

*F*AIL-PROOF OPENING LINES

- How do your know our hosts?
- Are you doing anything special for the weekend?
- Did you read that recent *Times* article about ____?
- Have you had time to catch that new George Clooney movie?
- Isn't this a great party? Do you know many people here?
- What a lovely ring. Is it an antique? The craftsmanship is exquisite.
- Did you get hooked on *The Real Housewives of New York City*? I hear they are working on another season.

Once you get the ball rolling, there are an infinite number of neutral subjects you can discuss—sports, travel, local events, hobbies, and trends, to name a few. This is where being well-informed with a broad range of interests pays off. A brilliant conversationalist can talk on almost any subject. But don't be self-absorbed. All you have to do is ask questions. Ask and you shall receive. A lot of the time, people are afraid to

> Whatever you do, don't start a conversation by asking, "What do you do?"

ask questions. Your curiosity and interest in the opinions and experiences of others are what fuels a conversation. There is nothing more charming than your sincere interest and undivided attention.

Of course, a conversation isn't one-sided—it takes two to tango. The responsibility is not entirely yours.

A GOOD CONVERSATIONALIST

The primary quality of someone with a gift for conversation is the ability to listen. You should look the other person in the eye. Don't scan the room or look over someone's shoulder to watch other guests arrive. If someone has ever done that to you, you know how awful it feels to become invisible. An elegant person makes the person she is talking to feel as if he's the only person in the room. You should nod during a conversation to indicate you understand and appreciate what is being said. You should try to make even the dullest person feel fascinating and significant or move on quickly.

> Don't make others the objects of your wit.

I always go to a party with a few jokes up my sleeve. A good joke can liven up any conversation, and everyone enjoys a good laugh. It's a pleasure to hear people having a good time. A quick wit is always charming, but a joke will do as well. Be aware that a dry wit can seem mean and bitchy. Don't make others the objects of your wit. You certainly don't want your humor to be misinterpreted. Old friends should be able to tease each other.

Having grown up in a large family, I'm used to verbal sparring. We tormented each other relentlessly. My older brothers teased me about girly things. I remember leaving for vacation with my parents and wanting to stay behind with my brothers. Of course, they couldn't wait for us to leave the house so that they could have a party. They certainly didn't want their little sister spying on them.

CONVERSATION KILLERS

- **Talking too much about yourself**—The idea is to get out of yourself and connect with someone else.

- **Complaining about your problems**—Nobody likes a downer. The loss of your job or your recent breakup will not make for sparkling conversation.

- **Bad breath**—Have Tic Tacs on standby.

- **Going on and on**—Don't tell long stories or be long-winded. Keep your contributions short and crisp. There's a reason it's called chitchat.

- **Getting too personal**—Asking "How old are you?" is the worst. You can tell if you're prying by the evasive answers you get. Similarly, don't talk about your personal assets, salaries, bonuses, or what something costs.

- **Giving advice**—unless it's asked for.

- **Telling racial jokes**—Expressing prejudice about race, religion, nationality, or politics is unattractive, not edgy.

- **Bragging**—Modesty is essential to elegance. You don't have to try so hard to impress.

- **Being negative**—Putting a damper on good spirits is never appreciated.

- **Overcomplimenting**—Insincerity can be painful to listen to.

Listen to Yourself

Learn from your mistakes. From watching myself on Season One of *Real Housewives,* I realize I say "you know" a lot. My husband often draws my attention to it. Be aware of any distracting verbal habits you might have. Don't mutter or rely on slang or clichés. We are often unaware of words and sounds we use that pepper our speech—like, um, you know, uh, actually. Realizing what you are doing is half the battle. You can consciously try to remove these "fillers" from your speech. Breathe in when you pause while talking instead of making that sound or saying that word. An inhalation will replace fillers.

Another thing to look out for is repeatedly using the same adjectives—*unbelievable, awesome, incredible, terrific, great, beautiful, fabulous, cool.* If these words are used too often, they lose their meaning. The word I overuse is *darling*, darlings. I think Honeychile got me stuck on it since she was from the South. People's expressions often rub off on us before we realize it.

When to Change Direction

Occasionally, conversations veer far off course. When you feel an argument brewing, you might want to change the subject. If you can deflect a conflict, you have done a good deed by saving people the embarrassment of losing their tempers.

I am a bit unorthodox on this point. In some groups, discussing religion and politics—generally forbidden—can result in a lively conversation, an intellectual exercise that offends no one. Why are people so afraid to talk about religion and politics?

> There is no conversation more boring
> than the one where everybody agrees.
> —*Michel de Montaigne*

The fun of the *Real Housewives* to me is that we are all different, and we don't always agree. I guess that's what makes it interesting to watch. I usually play the referee. They call me Miss Switzerland, because I always try to stay neutral. No one wants to brawl at a social gathering—unless you're shooting the *Housewives* show.

Sometimes people get carried away with their expert knowledge or passion, and the conversation gets out of hand. If the discussion gets too erudite and you can see others are not that interested, you will be doing everyone a favor by changing the subject.

If someone makes a faux pas, shift the conversation away from the embarrassing situation as gracefully as you can. Let's say someone asks an acquaintance in your presence, "How is your wife?" and the couple just had a nasty divorce, you can step in and say something light, like "He hopes far away. They've divorced recently." I often say, "Are we happy about that or are we sad about that?" That way you direct the focus away from the blunder and give the divorced friend a chance to recover. If you asked the embarrassing question and the person you are talking to fills you in, just apologize and change the subject. "I'm sorry to hear that. I had no idea. Would you care for a drink?"

*C*OMPLIMENTS WELCOMED

Most people give so few compliments. A sincere compliment can brighten any occasion—so be generous with them. A compliment works wonders when a conversation stalls. Compliment someone on anything that attracts your attention—beautiful earrings, wonderful food, lovely flowers, the décor, a radiant smile or infectious laugh, an accomplishment or honor you've heard about. Your aim is to make people feel good. It doesn't cost anything, and you'll be surprised by the positive effect compliments have on people.

> I can live for two months
> on a good compliment.
> —*Mark Twain*

There is a fine line between a compliment and flattery. If you go overboard, your sincerity will be in question, and you can make the recipient of your appreciation feel awkward. Serial compliments seem desperate and are embarrassing. Don't overdo it. One thoughtful compliment will do magic. It's great when your words make someone glow.

Accepting a compliment is an art. Don't brush one off with an attempt at modesty. Responses like "This old thing?" or "It was nothing" or "I think I overcooked it" stop a conversation dead in its tracks. By dismissing a compliment, you are really questioning the taste of the person who bothered to express admiration. Instead, you should accept the compliment with a warm thank-you, saying, "How nice of you to say so" or "I'm glad you think so."

You can expand your thank-you in a way that keeps the conversation going:

- ❧ Thanks. I found these earrings in a vintage boutique. They had so many unique things.
- ❧ You are so kind to notice my new haircut. It's taken me a while to get used to it.
- ❧ Look who's talking. You've obviously been spending time at the gym.
- ❧ I'm so glad you enjoyed the apple pie. It's my sister-in-law's recipe, and we picked the apples ourselves.

The Tact Challenge

There is a certain type of question that can make you stop in your tracks. For example:

- ❧ Do I look fat in this?
- ❧ Did you think my speech went on too long?
- ❧ Was the curry too spicy?
- ❧ Do you notice what I've changed in the living room?

Honesty is important in conversation, but there are times when half-truths are necessary to avoid hurting someone's feelings—not to mention incurring their wrath. You can be more straightforward with your best friend. After all, that's what friends are for. Though we depend on our friends for the whole truth, a little humor can take the sting out. Tact is necessary with everyone else.

This is where the little white lie—or avoiding a direct

answer—comes in handy. Try to come as close to the truth as you can:

- ❧ I think you look slimmer in the black jersey dress. The floral pattern is beautiful, but it is so bold it makes a big statement. Or, The length of the skirt is perfect, but it might look better with a sweater than a tucked-in blouse.
- ❧ The speech was filled with clear information—almost more than I could absorb.
- ❧ The curry was so exotic. That yogurt sauce was a perfect balance to the spiciness. That was so clever of you.
- ❧ This room is a feast for the eyes—it has such balance. I always feel so at home in it. You've changed something, but I just can't pinpoint what it is.

Being diplomatic takes practice. You can find something worth complimenting in any situation and can mask a criticism with a helpful suggestion. That's the best way to sidestep those hard-to-answer questions.

When You Are on the Receiving End

If someone commits a faux pas, stay cool and pleasant. Fill the person in quietly, and say after the person apologizes, "Please don't feel bad—how would you know? We've kept it quiet," or any comment that would get her off the hook. Then change the subject.

If someone insults you or your taste, say, "I'm surprised to hear you say that." Or, "I'm sure you didn't mean to offend me." Or, "That's a new take on things." Or, "I've never known anyone who feels that way." Keep it crisp, then accept any apology offered. Don't end the conversation abruptly, even if you are dying to run in the other direction.

Sidestepping Personal Questions

We have become so accustomed to people discussing the most intimate details of their lives on radio and television talk shows, in magazine interviews, and in tell-all memoirs that it's no wonder the boundaries defining what is private have blurred. At best, those boundaries are relative. You have a perfect right to define your comfort zone. You'll just have to develop your non-answers. If someone asks you how much something costs, you can always say, "I really don't know. It was a gift." Or there is the ever-useful "I don't remember."

If the questions or comments are rude, you can smile and say in a light tone, "I just don't think I'm going to respond to that." Or my favorite, "Oh, I'd have to know you a lot better to answer that!"

Sometimes people might ask you tactless or impertinent questions, meant to throw you off balance. In those cases, have a little fun and toss it right back. "Wherever did you hear that?" or "I'm sure you could give me some advice on that."

There is no reason to put up with prying questions. By handling the situation smoothly, you can let it be known that you are not amused, without causing friction.

How to Disagree Politely

You have to tread carefully when you are dealing with differences of opinion. Open-minded people can discuss anything without tempers flaring. The attitude with which to approach a disagreement is the desire to understand a different point of view in a nonjudgmental way. When you start judging, you stop listening.

Avoid blunt statements like "That's wrong!" or "You can't be serious!" You can express your reaction with more tact by saying, "It seems to me . . ." or "I disagree with you on that" or "there are other ways to interpret what happened."

It's always courteous to **ask questions to clarify the point.** For example, you could ask, "Where did you hear that?" or "How did you arrive at that conclusion?"

It's often helpful to **restate what the person has said**—"So, in your opinion . . ." or "Do you mean that . . ."

If you want to **express an opinion by acknowledging the other position,** you can say, "I understand what you are saying, but I have observed . . ." Or "There are other ways of looking at the issue."

A conversation is a chance to express an opinion. Your goal is not to convince someone else to accept your point of view. Nobody likes a know-it-all. If the exchange becomes heated or the person with whom you are talking becomes overbearing and tries to change your mind, you can just say, "Let's agree to disagree on that. It was interesting to hear what you think about . . ." Or "Thanks for sharing your thoughts with me. I'll have to think about that."

Gossip Girls

Everybody loves to gossip. A city like New York runs on gossip. Gossip provides you with the "who's new, what's hot, what's not, what's about to be hot." It's buzz or word of mouth. Keeping your ear to the ground allows you to be in touch with what is happening in your town or city.

> I don't care what is written about me
> so long as it isn't true.
> —Dorothy Parker

I dislike bad gossip, because it's hurtful and not all that classy. It involves spreading lies, confidences, or intimate information about people that is better left unsaid. There is an entire industry of gossip in the media that often has only the most tenuous relationship with the truth. That sort of gossip is a destructive force in our society.

I try never to repeat anything that I wouldn't say to someone's face. I'd like to think that the people I know would protect my privacy and reputation in the same way. When a conversation begins, "Don't repeat this, but . . ." or "Did you hear the terrible news about . . ." or "You're not going to believe this . . .", you know what's coming. If you hear gossip about a friend, you can ask the people who have mentioned the "tidbit" not to repeat it.

If you don't want to hear what they have to say or don't like the horse's mouth it's coming from, there are many ways to cut off the conversation, including:

❧ I think I'd rather not hear the rest.

❧ I try to stay away from that sort of talk. . . .

❧ Do you think our friend would want people to know that?

❧ I'd prefer for her to tell me herself.

❧ That rumor has been going around forever. . . .

❧ I think it's unkind to repeat that. Let's not spread it around.

❧ I'd hate for people to talk about me that way. Wouldn't you?

When you're a public figure and you put yourself out there, it comes with the territory. You are a goldfish in a bowl. It's the law of compensation.

Ending a Conversation

If you are stuck with someone who is boring, pompous, bragging, or competitive and you just want to escape as cleanly as possible, then smile, put out your hand, and say, "I'm so glad we had this chance to talk. Enjoy the rest of the party." Or "Thanks for such an interesting conversation. I think I'll give our hostess a hand." Or "I don't want to monopolize you. I'm sure you'd like to mingle."

Some conversations reach a natural end, and you are ready to move on. You can say, "I certainly have enjoyed talking with you. Have you met Colin Massey yet? Let me introduce you to him." Or you can say, "It's been good talking with you. I'll think I'll mingle a bit and catch up with some other acquaintances."

At the end of a conversation, do not offer a business card unless you are asked for one. One way to get around this is to say, "May I have your business card?" Usually, the person with whom you are talking will ask for yours, too.

In my garden in NYC

(PHOTO BY MARILI FORASTIERI)

At Table

*Y*OU NEVER KNOW
WHAT CAN HAPPEN AT DINNER

I met my husband at a dinner party. Honeychile and I were invited to dinner at the home of our friends the Notzes, in Gstaad. As we made our entrance into the drawing room of the beautiful chalet for cocktails, Honey whispered to me, "Oh, look at him!" I glanced in the direction of her gaze and saw two very attractive men, who happened to be Alex and his younger brother, Ferdinand. "Forget about him," I said. "Look at who's next to him," referring to the man who would become my husband.

When we went into dinner, I was delighted to find that I had been seated between Alex, on my right, and his brother. I marveled at what a gifted hostess Brigita Notz was. She made an effort and had such a gift for putting the right people together. I was a very happy camper.

There were sixteen guests seated at that long table, boy-girl, of course, with every name card carefully placed and a dazzling array of candelabras, flowers, crystal, silver, and porcelain. Everyone looked so gorgeous in the candlelight, and the opulent dining room charged with an air of celebration.

The meal was served by the staple of Gstaad society, the waiters of the Eagle Club in their traditional Swiss dress did the party circuit in Gstaad, catering to Valentino, Roger Moore, Peter Sellers, and King Constantine of Greece, to name a few notable citizens. The waiters, the food, the ambience, and the company created the ultimate in elegance—what a dinner party should be—fabulous.

Alex had been introduced to me as Alexandre Count de Lesseps—and I had no idea what a count was. I had met princes and princesses and an occasional king, but I had yet to encounter a count. He was gorgeous and worldly—his conversation was sophisticated. We talked about skiing, life in Europe, and mutual friends.

We were captivated by each other. I felt as if I had stepped into an enchanted dream. And it all started at that dinner table.

WHERE HAVE ALL THE MANNERS GONE?

In our fast-food, take-out culture, many families rarely sit down together for a meal, and the cloth napkins come out only for holidays. Table manners have gone the way of fine china, sterling silver flatware, and finger bowls. They are taken out of storage just for special events. Children are growing up with little exposure to table manners, and adults have forgotten the lessons they learned at their grandparents' tables. I know this is true, because so many people write to me asking for guidelines to clear up their confusion.

Just as the way you carry yourself telegraphs a great deal about you, your table manners create an indelible impression. So much of social life revolves around food—whether you are at a casual meal with friends, a restaurant, or a formal state dinner. There is no reason for you to be insecure about what fork to use, whether you should use a spoon, or which bread plate belongs to you. Consider this chapter a crash course in table manners. I promise to make it as painless as possible.

NAVIGATING THE SEA OF GLASS AND SILVER

It can be intimidating to sit at a dinner table, because every hostess does something different. At a formal dinner, your place setting might make it appear that you will be eating forever, given the number of glasses and forks and spoons. The rule of thumb is to use the silverware from the outside in. When in doubt, see what your hostess or other guests are doing. If you are uncertain about whether to use a fork or a spoon, all you have to remember is this: When food is served on a plate, use a fork; when in a bowl, use a spoon.

Remember: Your butter plate is on your left, and your water goblet is on your right. It can be confusing if the place settings are close, which often happens at round tables that seat eight to ten. Another guideline: Solids on the left and liquids on the right.

> # Solids on the left and liquids on the right.

Formal Place Setting

THE HISTORY OF THE FORK

Though the two-tine fork was used in ancient Greece to hold meat when cutting it, forks weren't generally used for eating until the modern ages, because of superstition. A Byzantine aristocrat married the future doge of Venice. She would not eat with her hands, and instead used a golden fork she carried with her as forks were used by the wealthy in the Middle East.

The Venetians considered it decadent. The princess died soon after, and a cardinal called the fork diabolic and useless since spaghetti was hard to eat with it. The fork disappeared from the Italian table for three hundred years. The fork became popular as people became more aware of cleanliness.

When Catherine de Medici married King Henry II of France in 1533, she made forks fashionable in the French court. Guests would bring their own forks and spoons to dinner.

An English traveler named Thomas Coryate brought the fork to England after visiting Italy in 1608. He was mocked, but Charles I of England declared that "it is decent to use a fork." Some believe that was the beginning of table manners.

In the eighteenth century, King Louis XIV of France still used his fingers and a knife to eat. Once he realized how useful a fork was, he became the first host in Europe to provide sets of dinnerware for his guests. With the help of Cardinal Richelieu, he changed the shape of dinner knives by rounding the point, since they were no longer needed to prick a piece of food or to kill a dinner companion.

It wasn't until the nineteenth century that metallic forks became affordable to the rising middle class, who wanted to emulate the nobility.

NAPKIN FINESSE

Big napkins are so chic—for me, the bigger the napkin, the more elegant the occasion. There are so many beautiful linens. I love old linens—they get more luxurious with age. Switzerland, Italy, and France are the capitals of fine linen, and I probably acquired my passion for them there.

Napkins have an etiquette of their own. Here are a few guidelines:

- Once seated, wait for the hostess to put her napkin in her lap. If you are at a party with more than eight people, wait until those around you are seated.

- Unfold the napkin, then fold it in half, with the fold against your body. The weight of the fold will keep the napkin from sliding off your lap.

- If your napkin is in a napkin ring, put the napkin ring at the top left of your place setting. You will need to retrieve it later.

- If you have to excuse yourself during the meal, leave your napkin on your chair, indicating that you are coming back. At a restaurant, one of the servers will refold it and put it to the left of your plate. This will happen as well at a formal event with many attentive people to serve you. I have been to opulent dinners in Europe at which each guest had a liveried servant standing behind his chair to attend to his needs.

- During the meal, dab at your lips with a corner of the napkin to remove crumbs or sauce. You will not want to leave food on the rim of your glass.

- It's okay to cough or sneeze into your napkin, but do

not use your napkin to blow your nose. Excuse yourself
from the table or grab a tissue instead.

🌿 When you have finished the meal, place the napkin on
the left side of your plate, unfolded.

🌿 If napkin rings were used, pull the napkin through the
ring and place it on the left with the point facing the
center of the table.

𝒪N ELBOWS

- When you are not eating, your hands should be in your lap or
your wrists can be on the edge of the table.
- Despite what your mother told you about keeping your elbows
off the table at all times, it is acceptable between courses.
Leaning forward a bit on your elbows shows that you are listening with interest.
- While you are eating, keep your elbows and forearms off the
table. Trying to eat with your elbows on the table is clumsy.
- Keep your elbows close to your sides while eating. You do not
want to become a hazard to your dinner partners.

𝒜 VOTRE SANTÉ—NO CELEBRATION IS COMPLETE WITHOUT A TOAST

Wait to drink your wine at a dinner table to see if a toast will be
given. In Europe, the host traditionally toasts his guests, welcoming them to his home. At informal meals, a guest often toasts the
host and hostess first to thank them.

All glasses have to be filled before a toast is made. It doesn't matter what beverage is used to toast with. It is acceptable for nondrinkers to toast with water or whatever they are drinking. In Europe, it's considered bad luck to toast with water, though. If you find yourself in that situation, raise your glass, but don't click glasses. It's taboo. The toaster takes a sip from his glass, then everyone else does, too, repeating the short form of the toast—"To our hosts"—or saying, "Hear, hear" or "Cheers."

I love to toast in other languages—*chin-chin, salut, santé, à votre santé, arriba.* And I like to keep it simple and sweet. A German friend of mine was known for his toasts; they would go on and on. Sometimes he would hit it right, but often his toasts were long-winded "there he goes again" affairs—the toasts that never ended.

Jean-Claude Sauer, a war photographer for *Paris Match,* invited us to his hunting lodge in the French countryside. At the dinner table, Jean-Claude made a toast in French that I'll never forget:

"Go where you like, because you will die where you're supposed to."

When you click glasses, make sure you look into the other person's eyes. It gives the moment significance.

Spontaneous toasts bring appreciation and joy to a gathering. They don't have to be profound—just heartfelt.

$\mathcal{O}$N BEING SERVED

When you are not served an individual portion, you will have to serve yourself from a platter. The server should approach you from the left side, but don't count on it. Have you ever tried to serve yourself from the right? It's practically impossible!

The platter will have a fork and a spoon for serving. Take the portion closest to you. Make sure you put the serving utensils back together on the serving platter.

$\mathcal{W}$HERE TO PUT CONDIMENTS

- Salt and pepper stay together and are passed together.
- Spoon gravy from the gravy boat directly onto meat, potatoes, or rice.
- Condiments like mustard, ketchup, mayonnaise, pickles, and jelly should be put on the dinner plate alongside the food.
- Radishes, olives, and nuts should be placed on your bread plate, or on the edge of your dinner plate if there is no bread plate.

If you don't like some of the food being served, take a small portion. You can pretend to have eaten it by spreading it around a bit on your plate. Even if you eat only a couple of bites, take some food. You don't want to offend your hosts or disrupt the party with your special needs. You can munch when you get home.

If you are allergic to something being served, do not bring attention to the fact that you cannot eat the dish. If your condition is too sensitive even to have a bit on your plate, quietly pass on the dish.

Family-Style Serving

When bowls and platters are being passed around the table, always pass to your right—that keeps the flow from becoming chaotic. Hold the platter for the person on your right while he serves himself.

*W*HEN TO START EATING

A party of eight or fewer. Wait for your hostess to begin before you start to eat.

A hosted table at a gala event. Do not begin eating until the entire table is served.

A mixed table. Introduce yourself to the people sitting near you and as others arrive. It is fine to begin eating when the people around you have their food.

A big banquet. As long as the guests on either side of you have their food, you can begin.

A buffet. You can eat as soon as you sit.

$\mathscr{A}$MERICAN VS. CONTINENTAL EATING

One of my dear friends had traveled to Europe for the first time, and my husband's father invited him to dinner at his home in Switzerland. I noticed he held his fork in a clenched fist—like a caveman ready to stab his food. I wanted to prevent him from embarrassing himself for the rest of his stay. So I taught him about holding a fork as he would a pencil and the fine art of using a knife and fork European-style. That's what friends are for! Remember, people do judge you by the way you hold your knife and fork.

The United States is the only country that does "zigzag" eating, shifting the fork from the left hand, which holds the fork tines down for cutting, to the right, after the knife has been placed on the side of the plate, to spear a piece of meat and bring the food to the mouth with the tines up. Sounds complicated, doesn't it? Switching back and forth seems like a waste of energy to me—and it could lead to a lot of clanking when the knife is rested on the plate.

Once you lift your utensils from the table, they never go back on. They stay on your plate.

The continental style of eating is more streamlined. The fork is held in the left hand, tines down, and the knife in the right. They stay that way though the meal. The knife, remaining in the right hand, is held low to the plate between cuts and not placed on the plate. The fork remains tines down as the food is brought to the mouth. The knife can be used to help get food onto the fork. Once you become accustomed

> Once you lift your utensils from the table, they never go back on. They stay on your plate.

to eating this way, it's a lot easier. It's like learning how to use chopsticks.

How to Break Bread

- To begin passing the bread, pick up the bread basket and offer it first to the person on your left. After that person takes a piece, help yourself to one and pass the basket to your right.

- Take an entire piece of bread, roll, or breadstick and place on your butter plate, or on the left side of your dinner plate if you are without a butter plate.

- Put butter on your butter plate rather than directly onto the bread. Take enough butter for the entire piece of bread.

- Break off a bite-size piece—never cut a roll with a knife. If crumbs fly, pick them up with your fingers and put them on your plate. Do it nonchalantly—not as if you are a busboy or waiter.

- Butter each piece as you eat one.

- A hot muffin or biscuit can be cut in half and buttered so that the butter will melt.

- A popover should be opened, buttered, and eaten in small pieces.

The Resting and Finished Positions

While eating, you should only do one thing at a time—kind of like driving. Your knife and fork should be put in resting position between bites or when you raise your napkin to your lips. If you want to take a sip of wine, put your flatware down. If you are having an extended conversation, don't hold your eating utensils in your hands. People might think you're armed and dangerous.

There is one resting position for both American and Continental styles:

Resting Position

When you are finished with your meal, your knife and fork should be placed in finished position:

Finished Position

When your silverware is in this position, you are signaling to your server that you have finished eating and your plate can be cleared.

EATING FAUX PAS

1. **Cutting food all at once, baby-style.** Cut one bite at a time. Your food will stay warmer, and you don't want to look geriatric!

2. **Seasoning food before tasting.** It's considered an insult to the cook. If you want more salt after tasting the dish, go right ahead.

3. **Lowering your mouth to the plate.** It's a good idea not to be a sloppy eater, but all you have to do is bend slightly from the waist to position your mouth over the plate.

4. **Making clanking or scraping noises with your knife and fork—like fingernails on a blackboard.** Try to handle your silverware quietly.

5. **Talking with food in your mouth (or taking a drink with food in your mouth and talking).** Take small bites of food. It makes conversation easier, because you can't always wait until you've swallowed what's in your mouth before talking. Don't risk looking like a chipmunk.

6. **Chewing with your mouth open, smacking your lips, slurping**—so unpleasant.

7. **Reaching.** Never reach in front of a person. Always ask for an item to be passed.

8. **Passing only the salt or pepper.** Even if someone says, "Please pass the salt," pass both the salt and the pepper. This is done so that these small items don't get separated from each other on the table. They're like an old married couple.

9. **Dipping bread directly into sauce on your plate.** It's irresistible, I know. But instead, put a piece of bread on your plate and spear it with the end of your fork. Then you can soak up some sauce and bring the bread to your mouth on the fork.

10. **Gobbling down your food or eating too slowly.** Try to keep pace with the table. You don't want to have to sit and watch everyone else finish, nor do you want everyone watching you chew.

11. **Picking up a dropped fork.** At a formal dinner or a restaurant, someone will replace it. At a more informal meal, you can ask the hostess for a fresh one or discreetly wipe it off with your napkin.

12. **Criticizing the food.** Never! You should compliment your hostess. In the past, talking about the food was "not done," generally because a cook prepared it. Now that so many of us take an interest in cooking, commenting on what you are eating is perfectly appropriate.

13. **Pushing the plate away from you when you are finished.** You are not Henry VIII. Even if you have feasted, keep your plate in front of you until it is cleared.

14. **Stacking and scraping plates at the table.** This is never done. Stacking and scraping turns food to trash before the diners' eyes. If you help the hostess clear the table, take two plates at a time.

15. **Drinking coffee or tea with the spoon in the cup.** Need I say more?

*D*ILEMMAS IN DINING

Being armed with the knowledge of the right way to deal with hard-to-eat foods and other nuisances will make your time at table an unabated pleasure. Remember Julia Roberts eating snails in *Pretty Woman?* You'll want to avoid flying food.

Difficulties with Hors d'Oeuvres
Since you are likely to be meeting people and shaking hands when hors d'oeuvres are served, always make sure you have a

cocktail napkin to keep your hands free of crumbs, salt, and other residue.

It's best to eat a canapé in one bite. Biting into one could cause collateral damage since you might splatter yourself or someone standing nearby. Before popping a hot canapé in your mouth, though, test it by touching your lip to it. You wouldn't want to burn yourself.

If a dipping sauce or hummus is served with shrimp, satay, or vegetables, hold the cocktail napkin under the hors d'oeuvre until it reaches your mouth. That will save your clothing, the chair you are sitting in, and the carpet from stains.

What to Do with a Toothpick

At cocktail parties, so many things are served with toothpicks. When you've helped yourself, do not put the toothpick back on the tray. Some caterers provide a food decoration on the tray that serves as a place to stash a toothpick. The waiter will indicate what is expected. Some people put bowls around the room for that purpose.

If you don't see an obvious place to put a toothpick, don't stick it in a plant or hide it in your purse. Wrap it in a cocktail napkin and leave it on a tray that is obviously for used glassware. Or you can go to the restroom and drop your napkin in the wastebasket.

How to Remove an Olive Pit

When olives are served as antipasti—as an hors d'oeuvre—you can pick them up with your fingers and discreetly remove the pit from your mouth with your fingers. You should have a place to put it—that's what butter plates or cocktail napkins are for.

When olives are in salads, use your fork to eat them and to

remove them from your mouth. Put the pit on the edge of your salad plate.

Socially Acceptable Finger Foods
You can almost count the foods you can eat with your fingers on one hand: asparagus, crisp bacon, the outside leaves of an artichoke, corn on the cob, chicken wings, and French fries.

Lipstick Stains on a Glass
Lipstick stains on a glass make me think of a crime scene where fingerprints are left. I have finally found a lipstick, made by Chanel, that does not leave a stain on glasses and lasts a long time. It has a clear gloss that you put on after the color to fix it. I love it. Frequent use of your napkin may help avoid a lip print.

If you are using lipstick that leaves a kiss mark on your glass, try to drink from the same spot to avoid having stains all around the rim.

Food Stuck Between Your Teeth
Embarrassing, but it happens to all of us, and it's always awkward. Take a sip of water and swish it around. Resist the temptation to pick at your teeth at the table if you feel something is stuck. Run your tongue over your teeth occasionally. Motion to a friend for a covert check. If worse comes to worst, you can excuse yourself and go to the privacy of the restroom. If it is impossible for you to leave the table, lift your napkin to your mouth and remove the food with your other hand. Do this as quickly and unobtrusively as possible—don't attempt major surgery at the table.

When Food Is Stuck in Someone Else's Teeth or Has Landed on the Chin

I'm sure you would appreciate someone telling you if you had a piece of very green spinach between your teeth, or gravy on your chin, so that you don't go through the meal oblivious. Do a friend a favor and save him from embarrassment. Don't say a word. Just get the person's attention and point quickly to your own teeth or chin. Look on the bright side—it might be a good way to initiate footsy. He'll get the idea. You will have done your good deed for the day.

Finding an Unwanted Surprise in Your Food

Oh, that sinking feeling. You notice a bug on a lettuce leaf or a hair in your mashed potatoes. As queasy as these finds may make you feel, do not overreact and trouble other guests. If you are at a restaurant, you can talk quietly to your server and let him handle it. At someone's home, it is best to move the offending part of the serving to the side of your plate, eat around it, or just stop eating. It depends on how much the mystery matter bothers you.

Removing Bones and Gristle

Gristle should be removed with your fork and placed on the side of your plate. Small bones from fish are easier to remove with your thumb and forefinger. The idea is to do this as discreetly as possible. If it is easier to remove the offending bit from your mouth with your fingers, do so. If you really don't like the way something tastes, swallow it as quickly as possible. I always hide it and camouflage it next to something else on my plate. Use your napkin only in an extreme emergency.

Serving Mishaps and Spills

My rule of thumb is to try to hide my faux pas, unless it's red wine on the white carpet. Don't try to sop red wine up with your white napkin. Ask for help. You don't want to get the reputation as "the spotter"—you'll never get invited again. A good hostess will understand.

If you drop some food on the table while serving yourself, pick it up with a clean spoon or your knife and put it on your plate. If you should drop food on yourself, dip a corner of your napkin in your water glass and dab at the spot. If food gets spilled on your dinner partner, don't jump up and pat at him with your napkin. Apologize profusely and offer to covering the dry-cleaning bill for your faux pas.

Chalet Oneida in Gstaad

(COURTESY OF THE AUTHOR)

The dining room in the chalet

(COURTESY OF THE AUTHOR)

7

The Hostess/Guest Connection

$\mathscr{A}$ FULL CALENDAR

During our years in Switzerland, I took great pleasure in entertaining at our beautiful home in Gstaad. Our chalet had a cozy dining room and was a perfect home for entertaining. The house was filled with antiques the de Lesseps had collected for generations. It was eclectic, but it all worked together—the Louis XV furniture, the Meissen porcelain, the Chinese antique collection from the far corners of the globe. I would often sit in the middle of the living room and relish the beauty of all the things that surrounded me. It gave me a warmth and tingle inside. The objects seemed to have a life of their own. I would wonder where they had been before and how many lives they had seen.

There was a fireplace in the dining room, and a studded, heavy medieval dining table that sat ten to twelve comfortably. The chairs were like medieval thrones, covered with animal hide. The furniture looked as if it belonged in a castle and had hosted countless banquets. I could only imagine the conversation that had gone around that table for centuries. The room had gorgeously crafted, recessed bookshelves, made by the Swiss, who are known for their fancy woodwork, to house the various collections—Meissen statues, boxes, monogrammed cigarette cases, antique silhouettes. On the table were huge candelabras, passed down for generations, which were so heavy they were hard to lift.

So for me, planning the meals was an occasion. From the setting of the table to the candles to the right dish to serve, it had to be perfect. I took pleasure in organizing the smallest detail of the evening. I enjoyed every minute of it.

Alex would organize the wines to be served—he loves Bordeaux—so he was always the sommelier. For hors d'oeuvres, I would serve goat cheese with olive paste on a water cracker, spring rolls wrapped in a lettuce leaf to protect the fingers, crudités. A typical first course would be foie gras, pâté, caviar, soup, or soufflé. I often served rack of lamb or duck à l'orange for the main course. Dessert was always a confection—chocolate mousse with orange zest, floating island, or a buttery pear tart.

Entertaining others is a generous gesture that requires time, planning, creativity, and thoughtfulness, but it isn't one-sided. The relationship between host and guest is a reciprocal one. Being a guest takes effort, too—it's not a free ride. If you are a fine hostess, your guests will be eager to reciprocate. And you don't have to be the life of the party, although that's what a good hostess likes.

Even last-minute parties thrown together are fun, sometimes the best because they are spontaneous. The first part of this chapter is about entertaining with ease and grace—about all the things that go into being a hostess whose parties everyone wants to attend. Being a good hostess comes with practice—believe me, it becomes easier the more you do it. The tips in this chapter will reduce the stress. When people arrive, you should be relaxed and have a champagne glass in hand. Then we shift to how to be a perfect guest—all the efforts of a hostess can fall flat if the guests don't do their part.

☞HE HOW AND WHAT OF CELEBRATION

You don't have to host a formal event to entertain your friends. Deciding what you are celebrating and how you are going to do so is the starting point. The more imaginative you are, the more likely your party will be memorable. Otherwise, why bother?

Time and money often determine what sort of party you are going to give.

An intimate dinner party with good friends is my favorite. but if you don't want to commit to preparing hors d'oeuvres and cocktails and a three-course meal, you can order in. Forget the cardboard and plastic containers—serve the meal you have assembled as you would a meal you had prepared in your own kitchen. I even know some people, who shall remain nameless, who have been known to pretend that the restaurant or gourmet-shop food they were serving *had* been prepared in their own kitchen. Why burst their bubble? Another way to accomplish the same results is a communal meal in which the host might be responsible for the main course, and each couple or guest contributes a dish or a course. I love it when people bring dessert, because I can't bake. It's a good idea to oversee the menu so you don't end up with a potluck nightmare. Sometimes it's fun for guests to gather in the kitchen and prepare a meal together—maybe a stir-fry or an exotic feast.

Perhaps you don't have the space in your house or apartment to entertain—that wouldn't be unusual in New York City. You could plan a picnic in the park, invite friends for dim sum in Chinatown for Sunday brunch, or reserve a private room in a restaurant. It doesn't have to be a four-star restaurant—local bars, pizzerias, Japanese restaurants, all sorts of places have rooms available for private parties. It's the thought that counts.

Of course, there are always traditional holidays and rituals like graduations, engagements, bon voyage, or moves away to celebrate. I made Thanksgiving in Switzerland and gathered all of my American friends who missed home. But you also might want to celebrate the first day of spring, a friend's promotion, the Academy Awards, the Emmys, A *Real Housewives of New York City* marathon, or a friend's return home from a long and exciting trip. You can celebrate just about anything if you choose to. Just be creative and have a good time.

Having a theme for a party pulls the guests together for a shared experience. If your guests have known each other for a long time, a theme can add life to an otherwise predictable gathering. If you are bringing new people together, a common purpose will unify the group. Party games can be fun—charades, trivia, karaoke, costumes, can all liven up an evening.

> Having a theme for a party pulls the guests together for a shared experience.

I used to have Halloween costume parties in Switzerland. Halloween is a nonevent in Europe, so people loved to come to our party because they got to dress up and be someone else for the night. It's amazing what happens to people when they put on a wig!

It DOESN'T HAVE TO BE DINNER

I once threw a birthday party for Alex's fiftieth that was one of the best parties of all time. The invitation was a book, and each chapter represented a different period in his life: Brussels as the son of an ambassador, Northwestern University in Chicago where he went to college, his years as a movie producer in Los Angeles, Paris, our marriage in the 1990s. People picked the chapter in his life in which they belonged and came in a costume representing that period. There were many pilots because of his global travel, and race car drivers, as he won the Tour de France in his Aston Martin DB4GT. . . . I, of course, came as his bride.

Alex's surprise birthday party
(COURTESY OF THE AUTHOR)

Brigita as Cher and me as Alex's bride

I blew up poster-size photos of him throughout his life and hung them all over the ballroom at the Palace Hotel in Gstaad. I seated people according to the years they belonged. It was a labor of love. Alex was overwhelmed to see the cast of characters from all walks of his life. His friends even got up and performed on-stage. John Sutin and Kirsten Gille did the Peter Sellers–Sophia Lauren sketch "Doctor, I'm in trouble." I hired a singer who sang all of his favorite songs, and I did my own version of "People Are Talking" by Bonnie Raitt. Brigita came as Cher and gave us her rendition of "Believe."

*D*IFFERENT WAYS TO ENTERTAIN

- A costume birthday party
- A wine or cheese tasting—people love to try new wines.
- A tea for your girlfriends—you can get perfect take-out tea sandwiches in New York or make your own.
- A card party—poker or bridge, depending on the crowd—with drinks and snacks
- Popcorn and a classic film night
- A Wimbledon, or whatever sport you like, party
- A costume birthday party
- A picnic on the beach or in the park
- A breakfast buffet/brunch with Bloody Marys or mimosas
- A workout party with a yoga instructor or a trainer at your home, and a salad lunch after
- A round robin tennis tournament at your local courts, followed by a barbecue

*I*NVITING THE RIGHT PEOPLE

Mixing people is always best—young, old, rich, poor, artists, Wall Streeters, people from all walks of life. You can have the best plans in the world, but if you haven't thought out your guest list, your party could be a dud—an experience you want to avoid, especially after the effort you've put into your party. Of course, if it's a big party, guests are on their own after a certain point. When I find myself at that sort of gathering, I just roll up my sleeves and go to work, introducing myself to people who look stranded and making sure they meet others. In such situations, a stellar guest becomes a subhostess. That's why you're invited. Be a social butterfly.

As much as I love big parties and to socialize, entertaining smaller groups is what Alex and I prefer. This way you can really talk and get to know people. If you go that route, you can be more exclusive about those you invite for each event. Your guest list can mix professional acquaintances, relatives, and friends. If you are inviting new people, make sure you keep the new guest at your side at the table. That will provide them with a comfort zone and make them feel welcomed. It's your job. Your list should balance old and new friends and people you'd like to know better. A roomful of people who demand the spotlight would be exhausting. A group of shy people would be equally disastrous. The secret to a successful party is a balanced guest list.

INVITATIONS
(OR THE PLEASURE OF YOUR COMPANY)

Invitations come in all sorts of forms today—a phone call, an e-mail note, an e-vite, a written invitation, a printed invitation. Your invitation should set the tone of the event and indicate the best way for your guest to RSVP. It's a good idea to declare your dress code—casual, cocktail, city chic, all-in-white—but as the hostess, wear that special something. People will know when they go to your party it's an occasion to dress.

- ❧ For parties of more than fifteen guests, sending out written or printed invitations is always chic, but the e-vite works these days as well.
- ❧ For big parties, invitations should be sent in the mail.
- ❧ If you make your invitations over the phone, it's thoughtful to give your guests an idea of who is coming, but it's not necessary.
- ❧ If your guest is single, you might want to welcome him or her to bring a friend, but make it clear that coming with a date is not necessary.
- ❧ If a guest asks to bring someone else—perhaps an out-of-town visitor—it's up to you, but I find it's hard to say no.

YOU'LL DEFINITELY HAVE MORE FUN
IF YOU HIRE PEOPLE TO HELP

I'm so lucky to have Rosie to help me. In a perfect world, everyone would have a Rosie. Through the years of hosting parties together, we work as a team to make our parties successful. If you can afford it, hiring people to help you is one way you can be sure you don't run yourself ragged and are able to enjoy your own party. You always have more fun at other people's parties because you don't have to worry about all the details.

You might be fortunate enough to have a friend who is a chef willing to help you prepare the meal in your own kitchen or a caterer to deliver a dinner you just have to warm up and serve. Having someone to serve dinner, clear, and clean up certainly adds an elegant touch and allows you to stay in your seat, enjoying the company of your guests. It's so much more fun to be a hostess and not have to jump up to tend to the details.

At a cocktail party or an event with twenty or more people, having someone at the door to take coats frees you up to give your guests your undivided attention as they arrive. This is where my son, Noel, shines. He loves to see the guests arrive and to help his mom out. Put those kids to work!

A bartender to make drinks and clear up used glasses keeps a party running smoothly. Servers who circulate through the party with trays of wine, water, or champagne or hors d'oeuvres can keep people from clustering around the bar or food tables. It's always hard to keep people away from the bar and to get them circulating.

You don't have to go through an agency to find help for a party. Reach out to friends who might have help, but don't poach. Try the wait staff at a restaurant, even the local diner. People are often looking to make a little extra money. If you have part-time household help, she or her friends might be willing to help serve at a party. And put your children to good use. Often, they love doing it. Why not get them comfortable in social situations early? And they can earn a little extra money.

*O*RGANIZING PARTY HELP

- Make sure to reserve the date and the time well in advance. If you wait too long, you could be out of luck.
- Agree on the payment. An hourly rate is what the service staff expects. Twenty to twenty-five dollars an hour sounds right.
- A caterer or cook will bill according to what and how much food is prepared. It is important to determine what the help will cost when you commission the food.
- Decide what you want done for you and what you want to do yourself.
- Discuss what the people should wear—dark slacks or skirt and a light shirt, tie optional, no jeans.
- Make sure the helpers arrive an hour before the guests so that you can show them where things are and discuss what you expect them to do. Take the time to let them know exactly how you want things done. Nothing is worse than a hostess who is visibly unhappy with the help.
- If a helper breaks something, do not expect to be reimbursed or to dock his wages. Just be gracious. Accidents do happen.
- Tip generously. If you're happy, you'll want to use them again.

*S*ETTING THE SCENE

Your guests are about to arrive. You've chosen the food to be served and the wine to be poured. Your kitchen duty is finished for the moment. You are well prepared. Now is the time to take a quick survey of the party room or rooms. The lighting should be low and flattering. Furniture should be placed so that people can flow without obstruction, yet plenty of comfortable seating should be available.

I love a room lit by candlelight. If you are burning candles, you should stay away from strongly scented varieties. You might want to have a scented candle in the kitchen to take away the aroma of the foods.

Make sure stacks of cocktail napkins are available. Coasters are for amateurs and the uptight. If you are using stemware, a coaster isn't necessary. When in doubt, rest your glass on a cocktail napkin.

Check the powder room to make certain you have fresh soap, a pile of guest hand towels, and paper guest towels as backup. I like to have a scented candle lit

> # Coasters are for amateurs and the uptight.

and hand cream on a shelf near the sink. Make certain there are extra rolls of toilet paper as well. It's nice to have fresh flowers or a single rose in the bathroom.

Music Calms and Stimulates

I like to sing, but I'm terrible at being the DJ. If you don't have a DJ, iPod compilations are great. You should arrange the music from soft to easy listening for cocktails and a little more festive for the meal. Music adds a lot to the ambience and creates the mood you want. You do not want to drown out conversation nor do you want only the bass to be heard over the party buzz. What's great about music is that you can turn it up to get the party started and can turn it off to hint that the party is over!

The Barefoot Contessa

I believe that people should be asked to take their shoes off only at a beach party. Some hosts ask their guests to remove their shoes when they enter the front door, Asian-style. It's why I have wood floors and many people choose stone or tile flooring for entryways.

Taking your shoes off can be embarrassing—and it happened to me. I arrived at a party to find that I was expected to leave my shoes at the door. No one had told me. The nail polish on one toe was badly chipped. I got resourceful, slipped away to the restroom, and covered that toe with a Band-Aid I had in my purse. I'm glad they were the nude kind and not Mickey Mouse.

You should tell your guests in advance if you will want them to remove their shoes. If you ask this of your guests, you should provide them with some sort of foot covering—Asian slippers or socks, for example—or at least have some at the door for people in need.

Be a Thoughtful Neighbor

My neighbor in the Hamptons sent over a bottle of wine, asking me to be forgiving of the noise, as she was hosting a party. I thought that was such a nice gesture. If you are having a large party or it might go on until the wee hours, you will want to let your neighbors know in advance or invite them. Telling them the date and the hours might give them a chance to plan an escape.

No Pets on the Greeting Committee

I have a friend with seven or eight dogs. When we arrived for dinner, they were lounging on the sofas, and you literally had to shoo them away to sit down. When I got up, I needed a lint brush to remove the hair from my black dress. That's why I like dogs that don't shed.

Aston, our West Highland terrier, is always around for small gatherings. If the party is larger, I'm afraid someone might step on him or that he will lick guests to death, because he loves skin cream.

Some people may have allergies, and others just might not like dogs or cats. If you are having a large party, your pets should not be wandering among the guests. Shut them off in a room.

Even pet lovers don't enjoy being jumped on or licked when they are dressed for a night out. We all know how expensive pantyhose are. Even if your guests are pet-friendly, they should not be treated to begging at table or pets sitting on furniture or jumping up to view what's on the kitchen counters. If your pets are just too sociable and your guests find them an unwelcome distraction, you might think about having a neighbor's child watch them for the night.

THE COCKTAIL PARTY

I went to a party not long ago and the hostess arrived late. The problem was that she was so busy getting her photo taken for the society pages that she ignored her guests. She wasn't there to make introductions to get the party going. We were left to our own devices. Thank heaven there was a bar! She looked like a goddess and the setting was beautiful, but without a proper guide, her party was a flop. A good hostess knows how to mingle and get the party started.

𝒞HECKLIST FOR A GREAT COCKTAIL PARTY

- Greet guests at the door. Here your warmth, enthusiasm, and personal welcome will set the tone of the evening.
- Take care of the coats. If you live in a small apartment, you might want to rent or borrow a coatrack from your building and leave it in the hallway. Make sure there are enough hangers. If you do not have enough space to hang coats in your guest closet, you can direct your guests to a bedroom where their wraps can be placed on a bed. If you have hired someone to help you, even better.
- Introduce each guest to someone upon arrival and talk about what they might have in common.
- Circulate and encourage conversation. A good hostess speaks with every guest and has antennae to find dead zones that need stimulation or people who are not mingling enough.
- Make sure that guests have replenished drinks. Whether passing hors d'oeuvres or suggesting a refill, a hostess is attentive to the needs of all her guests.
- Keep an eye on supplies—checks napkins, ice, glasses, hand towels and toilet paper in restrooms.
- Pick up used glasses, plates, napkins, and keeps ashtrays empty.

Cocktail parties are like making soup. You toss ingredients together and stir now and then as the flavors blend. There is less for you to orchestrate than a dinner party. A good cocktail party takes on a life of its own.

My husband loves to be the bartender at our parties. We like to serve a signature cocktail for the evening—Bellinis, cosmopolitans, martinis, margaritas. It makes the party feel more festive if a special drink is served. At least one bar should be set up in a place that is easily accessible. If you do not have a bartender, you can ask guests to help themselves. Be certain you have plenty of ice and that corkscrews and can openers are in plain sight. Nonalcoholic beverages, including mineral and sparkling water, fruit juices, and soft drinks, should be available for people who choose not to drink.

Make sure bowls of nuts, crudités with a dip of some sort, and munchies are placed strategically through the room. A small table or two, holding more complicated hors d'oeuvres, like cheese and crackers, shrimp and other shellfish, sushi, and pâté should be well situated to accommodate your guests. Small plates and forks will allow your guests to serve themselves. Remember those cocktail napkins.

Winding Down
(or The Guests Who Would Not Leave)

Sometimes invitations have a beginning, but the end is forgotten. It's flattering when the evening is such a success that people don't want to leave, but you have every right to wrap it up. It's easy to get the message across, if you send a few signals. You could ask, "Would you like a nightcap?" or "Will you have a cup of espresso before leaving?" You can start to tidy up a bit. Most people will get the hint. If someone seems entrenched, you can be direct. "Sally, I'm going to have to go to bed. I have to get up at the crack of dawn tomorrow," and say it with a woe-is-me inflection. If all else fails, close the bar.

A DINNER PARTY

A dinner party that I look forward to each year is given by our dear friends the Brandts during the Christmas holidays in Switzerland. They invite us to their winter *alpage,* a farmer's cow barn without electricity or heat. We drive up a winding farm road where only one car can pass at a time. We park on the mountainside and walk through the woods on a snow-covered path that is dimly lit by torches. Bundled up, we have the Swiss equivalent of mulled wine, air-dried meats, and local Swiss cheese in the moonlight.

The farmhouse is lit by candlelight and there's no running water. All the food is cooked in the massive fireplace. Cheese or meat fondue is usually served. Our host stirs the fondue in a big cauldron. It's like stepping back in time. It's so cozy and charming. There's something very intimate about the warmth created by our bodies, sitting closely together enjoying each other's company.

Dinners are my favorite form of entertaining—either as a hostess or as a guest. There is something wonderful about sharing a meal with friends. The pace is leisurely, and there is time for thoughtful conversation. Intimate dinner parties—eight is the perfect number—allow for the entire table to be part of a single conversation now and then, rather than restricting conversation to the people seated on either side of you. It's a younger, more contemporary way to entertain.

For a small dinner party, a balance of types and experience can be lively, but you want to achieve harmony. It's hard to escape a dinner partner—the man on either side of you is yours for at least two courses! As a hostess, you have to keep this in mind as you plan your table strategically.

Some hostesses make a point of asking if their guests have allergies to certain foods or health or religious restrictions about what they can eat. I don't feel it's necessary, and I think that guests should quietly deal with what is served to them. Vegans pose a challenge to any hostess—that's why meals should have veggies, a rice or pasta dish, and a salad that will work. I find buffets work well since so many people have weird food preferences and unheard-of allergies. But you can find many meals that have universal appeal. That's what being a good hostess is all about.

Cocktails Before Dinner

The evening should start with light hors d'oeuvres and cocktails, usually served in the living room. As guests arrive, the hosts take their coats and introduce them to each other. Cocktails is a time to mingle and become acquainted while waiting for everyone to arrive. It usually lasts about a half hour. If someone is late, I wait. I leave a grace period of fifteen to twenty minutes unless I receive a phone call explaining the delay.

The offerings should be light—nuts, crudités, wasabi peas—something light and crunchy works best. Traditionally, the host takes the drink orders, mixes and serves drinks to the guests, and makes sure drinks are topped off—though the hostess can act as bartender, too. If a woman or man has to keep an eye on the kitchen, the partner might want to take drinks duty. Offering a specialty cocktail can be a nice touch. If you have a pitcher of whatever you are serving, it will save you the trouble of mixing individual drinks. Wine or champagne should be served as well as nonalcoholic beverages. I always serve wine with dinner. Remember: Don't take drinks to the table unless asked to.

Creating the Menu and the Venues

Dinner is generally a three-course meal, with an appetizer, main course, and dessert, but you can be flexible about how you serve those courses. The appetizer can be served during the cocktail hour—maybe gravlax, shrimp, or caviar—and the guests move into the dining room for the main course. It's a bit more casual. If you'd prefer, your guests can move into the dining room for the first course, maybe soup, risotto, or salad. In Europe, salad is served after the main course rather than as an appetizer and can be followed by a cheese plate and fruit.

Dessert is an important course, because people tend to linger over it. I often serve mixed berries over ice cream with a touch of mint. It looks beautiful and it's light. It's a nice touch to serve little cookies, chocolates, or biscotti with espresso or tea. Offering a snifter of brandy is an elegant touch.

*M*Y NO-FAIL, PLEASE-EVERYONE MEAL

Potato-Leek Soup or Salad

Roasted Lemon Chicken

Basmati Rice with Roasted Pignoli Nuts and Raisins

Sugar Snap Peas

Sorbet and Biscotti

If you are doing the cooking and serving yourself, prepare as much of it in advance as you can. I do a lot of my own cooking, and I've collected recipes that don't keep me tied to the kitchen when I'm entertaining. Have the dishes you are going to need in neat stacks on the counter.

You can decide whether you will go from person to person with platters of food, pass platters and bowls family-style, or serve the meal as a buffet. It depends on how formal you want to be. You can ask a guest to give you a hand. People love to help. I prefer a casual approach. It's livelier!

The Joys of Buffet

Food is always a biggie for me, and I find buffets work very well for groups larger than twelve. It's an easier, more relaxed way to entertain. You don't have to worry about people's special needs when planning the menu. Your guests can pick and choose from what you've laid out. The most attractive thing about buffets is that guests are not stuck talking to someone while they are waiting for their food. Being able to mingle and to sit where they like is most welcoming.

SETTING THE TABLE

How your table looks depends on the meal you are serving. Leave yourself enough time to plan plates, glasses, and place cards. I show Rosie one place setting, and we set the entire table according to the plan.

> Light the candles before the guests enter the dining room, and remember not to use scented candles on the dinner table.

If you're pressed for time or help, set the table the night before your party so that task is crossed off your list. You don't need to be hunting for the soup tureen or Aunt Mary's champagne glasses the day of your party. You'll have plenty else to do.

If your dinner is to be on the formal side, plain white linens are always appropriate. But colorful linens, especially if they reflect a seasonal palette, can set the mood. Place mats on an antique wooden table or a slate table top can be elegant and modern, like accessories.

You can add all sorts of seasonal touches for your centerpiece—little pumpkins and gourds in the fall, pinecones and branches in the winter, pussy willow or cherry blossoms in early spring, a cornucopia of fresh fruit and vegetables in the summer. I use flowers from my garden. Use your imagination to suggest a theme for the meal. Just remember that floral arrangements should be low enough to see over, and candles should be lower than the guests' line of vision. Light the candles before the guests enter the dining room, and remember not to use scented candles on the dinner table.

$\mathscr{S}$EATING

It used to be that the number of women and men guests was expected to be equal—and hostesses were inevitably searching for that extra man to balance the table. The tradition seems to be going the way of finger bowls. I don't know about you, but I have so many divorced and unattached friends—and I'm sorry to say they are mostly women—that a strict observance of boy-girl balance is just not always possible. My husband travels all the time and my friends are happy to invite me to their parties by myself. For hostesses, it's a challenge, but they usually come up with some charming, single friends to balance their table.

How you seat your guests is a major factor in the success of a dinner party.

$\mathscr{P}$LACE CARDS OR NOT?

I appreciate hosts who put thought into seating their guests. It's a lot of work, especially if the guests are numerous. If you are having a small dinner party, you probably don't need place cards. When the dinner starts, the hosts enter the dining room first to seat their guests if place cards are not used. I find it easier to prepare an index card so I don't have to think about it when it comes time to sit. I've seen hostesses at parties with that blank stare on their faces. It's obvious they haven't put any thought into who will sit where.

If you are using place cards, the host and hostess enter the dining room after their guests. This gives you time to arrange the living room in preparation for returning to it after dinner.

You've set the stage for a terrific evening. Now you can relax and enjoy yourself.

LOCATION, LOCATION, LOCATION

- Try to seat guests with people they will enjoy or who are meeting for the first time.
- If you can manage it, the seating should alternate between men and women.
- If someone has never been to your house, sit him next to you.
- Seat an extra woman next to yourself.
- I always seat people who are amusing, and can carry the table, in the middle.
- Couples and close friends should not be seated next to each other (unless they are engaged or newlyweds)—they probably talk enough already.
- An elderly person should be seated to the right of the hostess.
- An honored female guest sits to the right of the host, who is usually at the head of the table. The guest's spouse sits to the right of the hostess.
- An honored male guest sits to the right of the hostess, at the other end of the table. His spouse sits to the right of the host.
- At small, informal dinner parties, there is often one conversation for the entire table. The hostess is in charge of the direction. When there is a lull, time for a joke.

OVERNIGHT GUESTS

In New York City, not many people have room for guests. I suppose that's why there are so many hotels. During the weekend, I like to invite my guests to the country. My guest rooms are rarely empty. My friends are always happy to be invited to leave the city for a weekend. You may have occasional friends and family members in town for a visit. This section contains simple advice to make sure the weekend is friction-free.

Making Your Guests at Home

Your guests may have driven for hours when they arrive, so let them put their bags down. Take them to where they will be staying and give them some time to unpack and freshen up. There should be hangers and empty drawers for their belongings. After they have settled in, walk them through your place and let them know how everything works. Maybe plan a tea or a walk to acclimate them to your setting. Depending on the season or time of day, I build a fire. Advise them of any quirks—for instance, if the handle of the toilet needs jiggling, where to put dirty towels, how to use the espresso machine, where to help themselves in the kitchen.

Give your guests a sense of your schedule—whether your household gets up early or sleeps in, when you tend to eat, and what has been planned. This is particularly important if your guests are sleeping on a pullout, futon, or air mattress in a public room. They should adapt to your schedule.

Plan to leave a hall light on at night in case your guest is a midnight rambler. If your guests have their own room, they might appreciate being able to sleep in if you are up at dawn. You can prepare their breakfast or leave a cold buffet so they can help themselves whenever they surface.

Most guests want to contribute and to be an active member of the household for the duration of their visit. Helping to prepare the meals—clearing the table, general tidying, or at least making their beds are expected trade-offs for your hospitality.

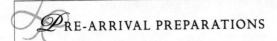RE-ARRIVAL PREPARATIONS

Sleeping Quarters—whether a separate bedroom, sofa bed, or futon

- Fresh linens
- A single flower
- Carafe of water
- Light for reading
- Tissues
- Wastebasket
- Books, magazines, local papers

Bathroom

- Bath towel, facecloth, and washcloth. Women often need an extra bath towel for their hair. Terry-cloth bathrobes are a luxury.
- Basket of shampoo and assorted toiletries
- Necessities that guests might forget—like an extra toothbrush, mouthwash
- Hair dryer
- Flowers

Extras

- Pencil and paper
- Extra pillows and blanket
- Safety pins/sewing kit
- Lint roller
- Sample perfumes
- If you really want to go all out—a chilled bottle of champagne

$\mathscr{T}$HE ART OF BEING A GUEST

Who doesn't love being a houseguest when there is a good hostess running the show? You can just sit back and enjoy without thinking about all the details—like what's for dinner and where you are going. A good hostess makes you feel taken care of.

Being an easy guest will guarantee many subsequent invitations. So go with the flow. Don't forget to acknowledge the effort and planning that goes into entertaining you. Being a perfect guest begins with your prompt response to the invitation. RSVP as soon as you can. Always ask if there is anything you can bring or do to help with the event.

Once you accept an invitation, your reasons for canceling should be unavoidable—an emergency business trip, a sudden illness, or a family crisis. We all know people who are serial cancelers.

If you receive an invitation for anything, never assume your children, especially infants, are included in the invitation. And that goes for pets too. If they had been, they would have been mentioned in the invitation.

I had a guest who brought her dog for a visit. I didn't even know she had a dog. Since we have Aston, it didn't bother me. The guest dog got into Victoria's hamster's cage and killed her hamster. Cedar shavings were scattered all over her room. You can imagine my guest's horror. She was mortified. At twelve, Victoria's response was, "That's okay—it's the dog's instinct. It's not its fault." We had a beach burial, after which my guest ran out to buy a new hamster. A word to the wise: Leave your pets at home.

If you have serious restrictions about food, you might want to mention the issue with your hostess if the group is small. If you know her well, she's already aware of the restrictions and will do her best to work around them. If you don't know the hostess well or the event is large scale, don't even bother to bring it up. Select what you can eat from what you are served. Try not to draw attention to what you are doing. Your hostess and the other guests will probably not be aware of what's on your plate.

If your religious beliefs might limit your participation in planned activities—let's say Christmas caroling—you might tell the hostess in advance that though the evening sounds wonderful, you forgot the words to "Jingle Bells."

Regrets (or How to Say No Graciously)

If there are real reasons why you can't be there, call with sincere regrets. Don't go into a deep, detailed explanation of why you can't attend. You should respond as soon as possible, so that your host can invite someone else in your place. Never complain or explain.

> **Never complain or explain.**

You obviously can't accept every invitation you receive, and you don't have to say why you are not accepting. You have to pick and choose your fiestas. Be honest, and if you can't be honest, be vague to keep your options open. If you are declining simply because you don't want to be there, simply say, "I'm sorry. I have other plans that evening." A prior commitment is an easy out. And you'll still be open to accept another invitation.

Be careful. You don't want to be caught in a lie. Duck if you see a photographer! Even though you've left your options open, you don't want to hurt anyone's feelings.

What to Wear

You've received an invitation, which is the best of all possible worlds. The invitation will tell you what to wear. If not, ask the hostess. If you remain puzzled, the simple black dress goes everywhere. As you already know, when in doubt, it is better to arrive overdressed—a notion worth repeating. You'll be an example of chic and elegance for everyone else at the barbecue.

Fashionably Late?

Fashionably on time is more like it. My husband is a stickler for punctuality. He is always ready and waiting for me at the bottom of the stairs—trying to rush me out the door. When the children were small, I'd be busy with finishing touches and would go for one last good-bye with them, leaning over them in their beds to kiss them good night. I knew my children would remember, years later, that I took that time for them. No one at the party would recall if I was fifteen minutes late, but my children would always remember me rushing out the door.

At a free-flowing event, like a cocktail party, many people choose to arrive when a party is in full swing—probably thirty to forty-five minutes from the invitation time. I don't think that's necessarily the best way to go. I like to arrive within fifteen minutes of the time on the invitation so that I can actually enjoy a conversation with the hosts before they become too busy. It's respectful to be on time.

If you have a full social calendar with many obligatory acceptances, you might want to arrive on the early side. This way, you can make your next event without being in a frenzy.

For a structured event, like a dinner party, you should be no more than fifteen minutes late.

Slipping Away

Honeychile and I spent a lot of time in Marbella, Spain, where parties started at midnight. Because she was older and wiser, she liked to slip away early, which could mean 4:00 A.M. Honey loved to leave people wondering where she was going—and with whom! She was so in demand as a guest, she could have triple-booked any night of the week. She was fearless and brilliant at radiating an air of mystery.

The Hostess Gift

It's nice to have something in your hands that puts a smile on your hostess's face when you walk in the door. I like to bring wine since so many of my friends have wine cellars. But don't expect your offerings to be served at a cocktail or dinner party unless it's a celebratory bottle of champagne and they ask you to pop the cork. You also should not arrive with a dish to be eaten with the meal unless you've discussed it with your hostess first.

If it's a casual dinner, flowers from the garden make a great gift. You can arrange them in a vase for your hostess since she'll be busy doing other things. For less than casual events, I think it is so chic to send flowers the morning of the event or a beautiful arrangement or orchid the day after.

Here are some of my ideas for hostess gifts:

- A fine bottle of wine
- Gourmet treats
- An orchid or plant
- A book you have loved reading or you know will interest your hosts
- Scented candles
- Hand towels for the powder room
- Kitchen gadgets
- A monogrammed beach bag
- A salad bowl
- A coffee table book
- Cognac or liqueurs
- An addition to one of your host's collections
- The complete *The Real Housewives of New York City* on DVD
- Soaps, bath salts, bubble bath, bath oils
- A cheese platter
- Sports-related gifts
- Exotic teas and coffees
- Fruit or seasonal basket
- Monogrammed bathrobe

*C*HECKLIST FOR THE PERFECT GUEST

- Respond to the invitation as soon as possible—no later than a week or by the RSVP date.
- Arrive on time—If you are going to be more than fifteen minutes late to a small gathering, call with the "I'll be there in five" line.
- Cancel only if it's an emergency—we know what those are.
- Don't bring a guest unless asked to.
- Don't be the last to leave, unless it's your BFF.
- Don't go to a party sick, even if you air kiss.
- Make an effort to dress well.
- Bring a hostess gift—don't arrive empty-handed.
- When you arrive, find the host and hostess first and say your hellos.
- Don't go into the kitchen unless the hostess invites you— we know how much people love the kitchen, but some hosts and hostesses don't like the distraction.
- Socialize with everyone. Your job is to help the hostess create a party atmosphere.
- Participate enthusiastically in any activities suggested by the host—party games and singing come to mind.
- Don't change place cards or seating arrangements at a dinner—and get caught.
- Don't open closed doors or take unguided tours—In other words, no snooping.
- Do not smoke inside if no ashtrays are visible. If you're a smoker, pray for an outdoor space.
- Offer to help your hostess during the party or with cleanup. (Hope she'll say no.)
- Thank your hostess for a wonderful time before you leave, unless she's on the dance floor.
- Call the next day or send an e-mail or note to thank your hosts. If it was a real shindig, send flowers.

The Wedding Guest

I understand why anyone would want a lavish, fairy-tale wedding. It's a dream come true for many. My take is a little different. Alex and I eloped and were married in City Hall in New York. I know that isn't the fairy tale you expected, but it couldn't have suited me better. I always dreamed of falling in love, being swept off my feet by a knight in shining armor on a white horse, and running off with him to live happily ever after. I wanted it to be just us, alone and in love.

Now so many people are having destination weddings in exotic places. They celebrate way beyond the wedding ceremony and the reception. In Europe, it's a three-day affair. However a couple decides to celebrate their wedding, there is a code of behavior for a wedding guest.

- ❧ Respond as soon as possible to the invitation. Your response should be handwritten. If there is not an RSVP card, you can respond formally, reproducing the layout of the invitation:

> *Mr. and Mrs. Robert Jones*
> *accept with pleasure*
> (or *regret they are unable to accept)*
> *your kind invitation for*
> *Saturday the fourteenth of July*

- ❧ If you have to cancel, let the hosts know immediately.
- ❧ Dress according to the time of the wedding—the later the wedding, the more formal the event. It's not a good idea to wear white, but black is socially acceptable these days.

- You should send a gift—an item from a bridal registry, or money can be what the couple needs most. It is best to send the gift shortly after the wedding.
- Arrive early for the service. It's fun to watch everyone arrive.
- Never move place cards—a lot of planning has gone into the seating arrangements. Major no-no.
- Introduce yourself to everyone at your table.

Overnight Stays

Just as a hostess has a checklist for entertaining overnight guests, you should be aware of what is expected of you as a guest. You are required to be adaptable—that's the primary rule. Your role is to fit into the rhythm of your hosts' lives. Of course, they'll take your needs into account, but in the end, it's their show.

CHECKLIST FOR A HOUSEGUEST

- Let your hosts know your plans for arrival and departure.
- Offer to bring whatever is needed—I always ask, "Can I bring you anything?"
- Bring your own toiletries.
- If you have young children who have been invited, don't bring snack food or drinks. They should have whatever is given to them.
- Arrive with a thoughtful present for your host.
- Pitch in during your stay—offer to help with cooking, dishes, and going to the market.
- Stay neat—keep your bathroom clean, make your bed, contain your belongings, and clean up after yourself wherever you land.
- Treat your hosts' things with respect.
- Be adaptable to your hosts' plans and enthusiastic about the activities they have planned.
- Adapt yourself to your hosts' sleep schedule. If your hosts turn in early, try to do so yourself.
- Always ask before you use something belonging to the host—the phone, a computer, access to the refrigerator or liquor cabinet.
- Give your hosts some private time during your visit—take a walk, nap, read, do some local sightseeing on your own. Your hosts aren't responsible for entertaining you twenty-four hours a day. And vice versa.
- Let your hosts know if you've used something up—tissue, toilet paper, or milk, for example.
- Offer to take your hosts out for lunch or dinner at least once or twice during your stay.
- If you break something, tell your hosts immediately. Send a written apology later and a token gift.
- Ask your hostess what you should do with the linens and towels you've used.

First visit to the Statue of Liberty,
presented to the United States
by the de Lesseps for France

(PHOTO BY TERRI GOLD)

The Gracious Child

$\mathcal{B}$RINGING UP BABY

You can imagine growing up as one of seven children and being broken in by four older brothers. Manners in our house were all about who left the spoon in the vanilla ice cream.

My mom did an amazing job; she was a total control freak and very organized. Even though my mother had numerous children, she always had a handle on it. She was the disciplinarian in the house—the one we would run from when we got into trouble. You could always tell by the look on her face that she meant business. She inspired a certain level of fear and awe. It's so important that children know who's the boss. Teaching us right from wrong was very important to her. I'll never forget all of us lining up before church on Sunday morning for her inspection.

When I was growing up, I thought I knew everything, as most teenagers do. Out in the world far away from home, I realized how much I didn't know. I was unprepared for the level of sophistication I found in New York and Europe. I had all the basics, but there were nuances far beyond my experience. Yet I stayed open to all of it—and absorbed everything I could, the way a young child would.

As you will see in the rest of this chapter, I run my family the same way my mother ran ours—the leaf doesn't fall far from the tree. Even the children of a count and countess need a firm hand, even more so, because they are in the public eye. My husband's upbringing was much more rigorous than mine. He went off to boarding school when he was eight and was raised by French nuns. The son of an ambassador was expected to behave impeccably. There was little margin for error.

We started by raising our children in Switzerland, and then moved to the United States, because my family is here. It's important to us that our children are grounded with family in the basics of consideration and good manners.

I'm just like every other mom who has the challenge of instilling good behavior in her children. We all want the best for our kids. Giving them a good foundation in etiquette and manners will smooth the way for them when they are out in the world.

*G*REAT EXPECTATIONS

When she was twelve, my daughter, Victoria, was invited with me to lunch in Florida at the home of my friend, a well-known Broadway producer. The mansion was monumental—marble columns and floors, sculptures, tapestries, and paintings, and household staff everywhere. Even the dogs were lavishly cared for—there was a doggy buffet for my friend's pets. Victoria, who does seem older than her years, was the only child at the table. I was seated to the right of the hostess and Victoria to her left.

I looked across the table and saw my daughter with that wide-eyed expression that said, "What am I doing here, Mom?" The conversation was quick and sophisticated. Every now and then, someone would include her, asking, "What do you think about that, Victoria?" I was proud to see how well she handled herself.

Then disaster struck—at least from Victoria's point of view. She spilled some couscous on the table. I wondered how she would handle the minor faux pas. Her confusion was obvious.

The hostess noticed Victoria's discomfort. In her deep, theatrical voice, she said, "Don't worry, darling. It happens to me all the time!" With that, she covered the minuscule mess with her napkin. The butler replaced the hostess's napkin and swept away the soiled one. Awkwardness averted by a kind and thoughtful hostess.

Later, I made certain my daughter knew how to handle a spill. Of course, she already did, but she was a bit overwhelmed by her surroundings. She didn't want to risk doing the wrong thing. My friend's light response put the situation in perspective for Victoria, who learned that no one is perfect and that the world doesn't come to a standstill if you make a mistake. And if you are aware that you've made a faux pas, it's okay. You try not to repeat it.

I think that, by the time children are ten or twelve, they should know basic manners. That is not to say that they will be paragons of courtesy at home. I'm always pleased when the parents of my children's friends tell me how well behaved my children are. You wouldn't know it to see them at home! They're kids after all, and home is a comfort zone. It's great to see that our nagging has had an effect and that they take their manners with them when they are out in the world.

It's all about expectations. If you expect your children to be polite, it will happen, but they have to see you behaving that way, too. "Do what I say, not what I do" just won't work. Young children learn by osmosis. Parents have to set an example. If you never eat dinner together at the table, how will they learn basic table manners? If parents aren't polite to each other, how does a young child learn? Kids are like sponges—it's impossible to know what they pick up. So be conscious of how you want them to behave and show them how it's done yourself. The way your children behave is a direct reflection on you. It's your diligence that really matters.

If you have a nanny or use a babysitter, it's up to you to train them about what you expect from your children. You might walk in on them having a meal to find the napkins on the table rather than in their laps or maybe they are eating with their fingers in front of the television. Make your wishes clear. Your children deserve the best training, because it will smooth the way for them later on in life. You can teach them table manners from the time they are out of the high chair.

WHERE IT BEGINS

If a child learns the words *please, thank you, you're welcome,* and *excuse me* at a young age—just as they begin to talk—that is the start of civility. Those words will stay with them and will define their relationships with others. Young children want to please. The approval they receive for using the most basic courtesy will shape their behavior as they get older. Little children are smarter than we think—they'll soon learn that having good manners delights people—and often gets them what they want.

Another phrase that is automatic to us is *I'm sorry*, but it is a major concept for children to grasp. It means they know the difference between right and wrong—a principle that is the foundation of society. *I'm sorry* should not be overused as an excuse, though. Be sure your children are sincere in their *I'm sorry*s.

I can never understand how people can allow their children to run wild or make a lot of noise in public places. So many people feed their children sugar to pacify them for a moment, and soon the kids are climbing the walls. Not only is all that sugar unhealthy, it eventually makes the children cranky and tired—a losing proposition for everyone! Paying attention to what your children are doing and keeping them entertained will go a long way toward avoiding this problem. If you can't control them on a particular day, pack them up and take them home. There is no reason to inflict a wild child on others.

*P*UT YOUR FOOT DOWN

We all know spoiled children when we see them:

- ♣ They whine and nag until they get what they think they want.
- ♣ They can't take no for an answer.
- ♣ They talk back to their parents.

My own children pick up on the spoiled behavior of other kids by how they speak to their parents. Victoria and Noel have both said, "I can't believe they got away with talking that way to their parents." If you let your children talk back, it never stops.

Kids need routine and structure in their lives, and parents who are not afraid to say no. They have to know that you won't back down even if they throw a tantrum. Only consistency on your part will convince them that you mean what you say.

I was always striving to please my mother, and Victoria is very much like me in that way. Boys, of course, take a little more work. All I had to do was look at Victoria sideways, and she knew she was in hot water. "Uh-oh, there's my warning." She'd get it and act accordingly. It didn't work with Noel. He kept on pushing and pushing until he got a reaction. It's tougher with boys.

If you say something, stick to your guns. No matter how hard they push, don't back down. Time-outs really do work, because they give a child the time to realize you are firm, and they are not going to get their way. They can regroup during a time-out. And you can think more rationally and try not to lose your temper.

Bedtime has always been difficult for Noel. He'll always beg, "Just five more minutes." Since he was such an early riser, I'd sometimes let him stay up a bit longer, assuming he'd sleep later in the morning. No matter what time he went to bed, though, he'd always be up at 6:00 A.M. He always says, "I was born at six, so of course I wake up at six." Now, there's logic for you! Getting back to a routine was obviously in order. Children need their sleep. Add a spoonful of sugar to insufficient sleep and you have one ornery child.

In my house, kids eat what they are served. I try to tailor meals so they'll be happy, of course. If that doesn't work, there are no food replacements. It's either eat what you are served or a peanut butter and jelly sandwich.

When my children attended school in Switzerland, they had to take two bites of everything served to them at lunch. I think that's a good rule for any table. Children can learn to try new things early.

We love to have dinner together as a family. Even though

Alex and I are often out to dinner, I always try to be with our children at mealtime. I nibble at whatever they are eating. I want to make sure they are eating what is served to them, behaving with good manners, and being respectful to Rosie. Even more important, I love hearing about their days. It is a good time to be together.

If you put your foot down early in your kids' lives and refuse to respond to their pleas, which I admit is not always easy, it will pay off. Your firmness now will save them later in life. You are not doing a child a favor by spoiling him.

Of course, discipline has to be balanced with praise for everything a child does right—doing chores, being polite, observing house rules. Positive reinforcement just about always works.

$\mathscr{L}$OOK 'EM IN THE EYE

A child who is not intimidated when meeting adults is already impressive. When an adult enters a room, a child should stand. As he is being introduced, the child should look the adult in the eye and shake hands. It's hard—kids are often shy or awkward, but by the time they are ten, they should be almost there. It took my kids awhile with the shy phase, but the more exposure you give them to greeting people, the better and easier it becomes.

A child should not call an adult by his first name unless asked to. I am always surprised by the number of young people who automatically call me LuAnn. It should be Mister, Missus, or Miss. It's up to you to decide how you would prefer to be addressed. Of course, a child could forget your name, but when a child makes that extra effort and says, "Hi, Mrs. de Lesseps," I automatically think, "Wow! What a well-mannered child." It might take some time for a child to develop the confidence, but when he sees how well people respond to his efforts, he can only feel good about himself.

A child should always answer when spoken to—not just mumble and look away or ignore what an adult has said. Showing respect for adults is always important. They should know to respect their elders and not to interrupt them every two minutes. Unless you tell them, they will not even realize they are interrupting or being rude.

CHORES AND RESPONSIBILITIES

When I was growing up, my mother could not have managed if all seven of us kids hadn't pitched in to help her around the house. Both my mother and father came from very large families, so they expected each of us to do our part. I used to supplement my meager allowance by ironing my brothers' shirts for one dollar when they had a date. They certainly didn't want to do it, and my mother was too busy.

I have the same expectations of our children. Having responsibilities builds character—it's good for the soul to have to deal with doing things you'd rather skip. It's hard to think of a better preparation for real life.

We had a chore chart when Victoria and Noel were little. We'd check off what they did, and they would get rewarded. They each had a pebble jar. Every time they did a chore or did something deserving notice, I would drop a pebble in the jar. For them, the pebbles were like gold. When the pebbles reached a marked level, they would receive a prize. Making a game of it worked. It became fun to observe a routine, to learn new things, and to behave well.

I expect my children to keep their rooms neat. Victoria has a hard time with this—so I asked the advice of a European friend, who could not get her daughter to pick up her clothes and put them away. She warned her child that if she didn't start to respect her things, she would toss them out the window, because someone on the street—maybe a homeless person—deserved them more than she did and would be thrilled to have them. And my friend followed through. When her daughter saw her jeans, boots, and sweaters flying out the window, she realized that she'd never see her clothes again. It didn't take her long to start taking care of things and picking up after herself, realizing her mother was not going to replace what she'd tossed. I haven't gotten to the point of tossing Victoria's clothes yet, but it is coming. . . .

I want my children to take care of things and to respect the order of the house. It's a sign of respect for other people. So kicking their shoes off when they come in the house for others to trip over, not hanging up their coats, or leaving their backpacks filled with schoolbooks out in the rain or misplacing them are all things that drive us crazy. They have to put things back where they belong—no spoons left in the ice cream or thrown out in the yogurt container or down the disposal. If they take the last can of soda or bottle of water from the refrigerator, I expect them to replace it. Glasses go in the dishwasher and snack wrappers in the trash. When they get up from the table, dishes go to the dishwasher. These are habits that they will take with them for the rest of their lives.

PLAYDATES

When their friends come, children should act as hosts. They should offer their friends something to drink or a snack. That might keep some kids from opening the refrigerator and helping themselves. I want my children's friends to enjoy coming to our home and to feel comfortable, but I don't appreciate it when they make themselves too much at home. There are boundaries that they have to learn to respect.

My children always have to clean up when their friends visit, whether it's a slumber party, the tent, the scattered toys, or a pizza party. It is their responsibility. Rosie is not an option. Of course, Noel complains, "But they played, too, and they didn't have to help." Over time, my children have learned to clean up before their friends leave, understanding that once the friends have gone, they are left to their own devices. I give them a ten-minute warning and suggest they straighten out together, not giving their friends a chance to escape.

MANNERS FOR PLAYDATES

- Say hello to the adult in charge.
- Do not help yourself to the fridge or cupboards.
- Don't wander about into bedrooms.
- Politely ask for a drink or a snack.
- Help to clean up.
- Say good-bye and thank you.

THE THANK-YOU NOTE HABIT

I know it's hard to get a kid to sit down to write a thank-you note, but the gesture is an important one that speaks volumes about how you are raising your children. They have to learn to acknowledge a kindness—whether it's a gift, being a guest at a professional sports event, skiing, the theater, an outing with a friend's family, or thanking someone for helping them get a job. Any written gesture will do.

I keep a stack of cards available—like when you send a child away to camp—to make it easy. They might get more involved if they can design their own cards online. An e-mailed card or note is fine, too. It's the gesture that matters.

Start young. If the entire family is giving a gift to someone, have your children sign their own names—even if it's an X or a scribble. Ask them to sign your Christmas cards. It can become part of the festivities. If you get them young enough, they will consider it fun. Correspondence won't be an alien form to them.

Teach your children not to write a rote note à la "Thank you for the gift." They can learn to personalize a thank-you note by writing, "Thank you for the beautiful sweater. It's my favorite color." Of course, the notes will be more sophisticated as they get older.

When my children received a gift in Switzerland, they would often call to say their thank-yous. If a grandparent or aunt lives far away, a phone call can be the best form of thank you—it's great to hear their little voices. If you are really busy and there's a chance that the thank-you note won't go out in a week, a call will do the trick until it arrives.

WHO'S CALLING?

Though most kids use their cell phones and text-message, they should be able to deal with answering the house phone. A simple "Hello" is a fine way to answer. You never know who is calling and may not want to give out your name indiscriminately by answering "Smyth residence."

If the caller asks for someone else, "May I tell her who's calling?" is an appropriate response. In this age of handheld phones, children have to learn that they can't stomp around or up and down stairs without covering the mouthpiece or putting the call on hold. There's nothing worse than being blasted by an adolescent voice.

Your children should take messages for you—and paper and pen should be near the phone.

Sometimes your teenagers' friends might call your home phone if they can't reach your children on their cells. Any call before 9:00 A.M. or after 9:00 P.M. is not acceptable. Your children should tell their friends about this house rule if they want to save them from the embarrassment of being reamed out by a parent.

BAD BEHAVIOR

Smacking Gum

If you can manage to keep gum out of the hands of your children, do it. Bovine chewing is really obnoxious. I was at a party with the daughter of a friend who was chewing away. I could barely stand to be next to her. Gritting my teeth, I said to her, "I don't allow my daughter to chew gum in most places. She just can't handle it. I know all girls do it, but it's better to chew gum in the car alone with the closest of family." Guess what? She took that gum out of her mouth, realizing her chewing was out of control.

Whispering and Telling Secrets

This is such hurtful behavior! But children are the cruelest. Kids should put themselves in the position of the person being excluded. How would they feel? In a threesome, a kid can only believe that they are talking about her. The only way to counteract this mean behavior is to have a one-liner like:

- ❧ Excuse me, I'm standing here. Oh my God, have I disappeared?
- ❧ What could you possibly be saying that I couldn't already know?
- ❧ Why don't you bore the rest of us in on what's going on?
- ❧ I'm sure I'm not missing anything important.

Children are so tender and it's difficult to see them have to deal with this sort of rudeness.

Heaven knows, I've had to supply my own kids with one-liners.

My advice to my children is to be an actor when bullied.

> **My advice to my children is to be an actor when bullied.**

Teasing and Bullying

Teasing falls into the same category. Children can target a sensitive person instinctively—they know who they can tease. My advice to my children is to be an actor. Don't wear your heart on your sleeve. Again, a one-liner can diffuse the teasing. Here are my suggestions:

- ❧ Act like you're extremely happy—and smile.
- ❧ Laugh and say, That's so funny! then turn around and walk away.
- ❧ Why don't you waste someone else's time?
- ❧ Don't you have anything better to do?
- ❧ Why don't you find someone else to be jealous of?

Noise Level

Since we live in a townhouse, there are many floors and no elevators. Yelling up and down the stairs can drive me crazy, so we've taken up calling each other on our cell phones if we can't talk in normal voices.

If a child wants to listen to or play loud music, a time and a place should be designated. If you can hear spillover noise from their headphones, remind them it's bad for their hearing. Thank God for headphones. At least the whole family does not have to hear blaring music.

Sometimes, sitting at a café on a New York street, I am astonished at how kids behave. Some walk down the street shouting, laughing loudly, and blasting music. Add that to the traffic and you can't hear yourself think! I realize that kids have a lot of energy—especially when they are first released from school—but how they behave on the street says a lot about who they are and how they are being brought up. Screaming, kick boxing, or catch are done in a park or in the privacy of your own home. The street is to be shared, and children should know to be considerate of other people's space.

WHERE DO CHILDREN BELONG?

I hate to say it, but the Europeans seem to have a better handle on how to deal with kids and their manners. I think it's all about children's respect for their elders. They dress to impress, extend hands to say hello, and actually look at you when they speak. Maybe it's because that's what their parents are doing?

In Europe, there is a clear separation between children and adults. It's the old adage "Children are to be seen and not necessarily heard." They know there is a place for adults and a place for children. Children in the United States are brought everywhere, which can be annoying. Who wants to pay a babysitter for an evening out at a fine restaurant only to be seated next to a wailing infant or a toddler throwing whipped

> In the end, it's not where you're from, it's about good parenting.

cream on the floor? Take them to restaurants that are kid friendly instead. In the end, it's not where you're from, it's about good parenting.

You have to be aware of what your child can handle. I know thirteen-year-olds who are like little adults. I love to take my children to openings at art galleries and good restaurants, because I want them to be exposed to those worlds and they can handle it.

You have to have a realistic idea of what your children are ready for. Some are more sophisticated than others. You have to take your cues from how they behave. Consideration for others has to be the measure of where you decide to bring your kids and what is age appropriate.

*I*T'S NEVER TOO LATE!

So, mothers out there, don't be discouraged or feel self-conscious about your kids. You can refine their social graces at any point in their lives. Just act the part and set a good example. I'm writing this book to give you the basics by showing you it's a learning process that never ends.

PART THREE

The Art of Seduction

A seductive shot from my modeling days
(COURTESY OF THE AUTHOR)

Alex and me at a gala

(PHOTO BY TERRI GOLD)

How to Get a Man to Fall in Love and Stay in Love

THE SIZZLE

I believe that all of life is a seduction. Life is unquestionably richer if you can get everyone in your corner, from wait staff to salespeople to the men in your life. Winning people over adds spice to life. It's the sizzle—and it makes every encounter special.

Seduction is the playful part of most of our relationships. A charming woman makes everyone feel important. An alluring woman makes everyone want to be near her. This part of the book focuses on persuading people that you admire and adore them while disarming them and convincing them that you deserve the best.

Obviously seduction works on many levels. You behave differently with your dry-cleaner than you do with the wife of an important man whose approval you need to get on their invitation list, or your husband of ten years, or a man you want to attract, or your girlfriends. Though passionate seductions are the ultimate, everyday seductions are also necessary. In The Art of Seduction, we'll consider the various degrees of seduction, from how to get a man to fall in love with you to keeping a relationship new to everyday seductions.

How to Get a Man to Fall in Love

The Seduction Was Mutual

After Alex and I met at that dinner party in Gstaad, we had a whirlwind romance. At dinner, he had invited me to go helicopter skiing with him. I accepted though I had never been helicopter skiing, and I wasn't a very good skier to begin with. I was terrified, but I was willing to go anywhere with him. I'm nothing if not adventurous—and I wouldn't have missed it for anything.

Much to my relief, he called the next day, apologizing that there wasn't room for me on the helicopter. He invited me to go to a party with him on Saturday night instead. Since I wanted to be not-so-available and was already invited to the same party, I told him I would meet him there. I was a bit miffed that he had broken our ski date—the one for which I had been willing to risk life and limb. I wanted to show him that I didn't need him to invite me.

Patrick Bruel, a well-known French singer, was the host of the party, and I was seated next to him. He was being very amorous. As I tried to deflect his attentions, I kept an eye out for Alex. I wondered if he had spotted me yet. Our table was up on a balcony that surrounded the dance floor. My heart sank as I saw Alex walk in with a tall Bavarian blond woman.

I was so disappointed that he had brought someone else after asking me. My playing hard-to-get seemed to have backfired. When I saw him head for the restroom a bit later, I realized it was my chance. I went to the dance floor and waited. When he emerged, I asked him to dance.

"Where have you been?" he asked.

"I've been upstairs being molested by our host."

I went on to ask him about the woman he was with.

"Oh, that's my ex-wife." I couldn't have asked for a better response.

We danced and didn't let each other out of each other's sight again. The funny thing is that when his ex-wife saw us dancing, she told his friends that I would be his next wife. Alex and I spent the following five days with each other, day in and day out. We skied together, had dinner with friends, and talked endlessly, getting to know each other.

I knew after five days that he was the man for me. Little did I know that he felt the same way. Even though he said repeatedly, "You know that you're going to be the mother of my children," I assumed he was joking. I think it's fair to say that the seduction was mutual.

Those five days were magic. As he is an accomplished skier, I would follow behind him on alpine trails, feeling that I was the luckiest girl in the world. It seemed as if we owned the mountain as we swished by the pines heavy with snow. I was utterly in awe and in love and admired him totally.

We met for tea at Charlie's after the big party. Alex said to me, "You know what—you're living the wrong life. You should be doing something else." He sensed that I wasn't as happy in Milan as I seemed to be. He knew that I was ready for a life change, and I was impressed by how well he read me.

On the sixth day, as we rode the chairlift up the Horneggli

mountain, he casually asked me to marry him. My immediate thought was "Okay, what's wrong with him? He's everything I've always dreamed of—there's got to be something wrong." But at the same time, I had never felt such certainty about someone. It had never happened to me before. I had met my match. I said yes.

When I had realized he was serious about me, I called all my girlfriends who might know anything about him, for second opinions. I discovered that he had been married three times before—for very short periods of time. I would be wife number four. But as I listened to these women, I realized that jealousy was coloring their remarks and that they probably didn't want him to be taken off the market. I viewed it as a challenge.

So I made the decision on my own, and I decided he was perfect for me. You always think that you're the one who can change the man. And I did. We've been together three times longer than all three of his previous marriages combined—fifteen years.

If I had allowed myself to be skeptical and to drag my feet, my doubt would have changed the dynamic. My lack of trust would have dragged us down. The timing could not have been better. I was on the verge of leaving Milan for Hollywood. I was at the top of my game in Milan, and my agent, who was well connected in Los Angeles, thought I should go to California. If I had had to give up something important to leave Milan, it would not have been as easy. The fact that I was free to say "I'm in love, and I'm going to go with it" had a lot to do with how magically it went.

We decided to go to Paris to attend a party to which we had both been invited. We were elated to be in such a romantic city— Alex's hometown. But when we announced our engagement, we were surprised by the way our friends reacted—though I suppose we shouldn't have been. There were men at the party who didn't want to see me get married, and, of course, many women who wanted Alex to stay single. We didn't want our moment to be ruined by jealousy, so we decided to elope.

New York made a lot of sense, because Alex had rented a house in the Hamptons to write his second book, an autobiographical novel he planned to call *The Last of the Individualists*. We decided to fly to New York to get married, mostly because we wouldn't have to wait. You can be married in New York in twenty-four hours.

I married Alex in New York City Hall in jeans and a blazer. We had picked out a wedding ring in the diamond district. The owner was the father of Alex's oldest friend, Ron Guttman. When he saw me, he said to Alex, "This is a five-karat woman, not a three-karat." I almost jumped over the counter to kiss him.

I knew we were meant to be together. Remember "jump on the train or you'll miss it"? I didn't hesitate.

By the way, he hasn't written that book yet.

Getting a Man's Attention

When I first moved to Milan, I shared an apartment for a brief moment with Julie, a model who was Miss Hawaiian Tropic. Remember the importance of a title—any title—in Italy? She was like Ginger from *Gilligan's Island*. Men could not resist her. When she walked into a room, tails would wag. I've never seen a woman with more sex appeal. There's a lot to be said for sex appeal, because it's what men really respond to before they get to pick your brain. Remember, men are primarily visual creatures.

One day, we were walking down the street in Milan together after a shopping spree, carrying many shopping bags. A man slowed down slightly as he was going to pass us on his motor scooter, reached out, and pinched Julie's derrière. This was the Italian way of getting her to notice him. She didn't have to do more than walk down the street for men to go gaga over her, but for some of us it doesn't come that easy.

Don't be afraid to be sexy or flirtatious. There is nothing wrong with having sex appeal. Be a woman. Men love women who are not afraid to express their sexuality. Of course, it has to be the right degree of sexy: alluring and not aggressive or obvious.

It's better to be looked over than overlooked.
—*Mae West*

Mae West was one of the original sex goddesses. I love her quick wit—her quips are legendary. She clearly was a woman who enjoyed the opposite sex. Curvaceous and bodacious, she started in vaudeville, performed on the stage in New York, and moved to Hollywood to become a comedian, actress, and writer for films in the first half of the twentieth century. Honey resembled her in so many ways. I admire their fearlessness and brashness, so they are both icons to me. I've sprinkled Mae West's great one-liners through this part of the book because her insights on the battle of the sexes is so relevant today. It's time for a Mae West revival. She was very much ahead of her time.

Women are doing so much today that they often forget their femininity. Julie was ultra feminine, and men just loved that. I know this is a controversial statement, but I believe there are not enough Betty Boops in this world. Some girls just want to have fun with their femininity, and that can be very appealing to men.

Don't be afraid to be soft. Men respond to softness in what you wear, how you speak, your scent, and the way you respond to them. Wear clothing that reveals you're a woman—flirty skirts, high heels, a little *décolleté*—a bit suggestive, if you know what I mean. When you go to the office, don't look like a man. As they say in France, *"Vive la différence!"* The way you move catches a man's eye—a swing in your step and a little "come follow me" attitude.

> I like my clothes to be tight enough
> to show I'm a woman . . .
> But loose enough to show I'm a lady.
> —Mae West

My roommate Julie was sweet and ethereal. She didn't have a worry in the world. She lived from one day to the next. For Julie, every day was a surprise. I was the total opposite of Julie. Her way of being was alien to me. I was more ambitious. I wanted to travel the world, work in television, and meet Mr. Right.

I was happy-go-lucky, but I did have a game plan. What I discovered is that, sure, men respond to sex appeal, but in the end, it's about the package deal. Intelligence, curiosity, and goals count a lot. The next phase of attraction involves a meeting of the minds, shared interests, things in common, dreams that lead you both in the same direction. That's all part of what makes a man fall in love with you. The best enduring relationships are often true friendships.

You may admire a girl's curves
on the first introduction . . .
But the second meeting shows up new angles.
—*Mae West*

With Alex and me, it was a *coup de foudre*, a thunderbolt, love at first sight. We couldn't take our eyes off each other. It was a magnetic meeting of two souls. I think sometimes these are the most lasting relationships.

How to Flirt

Flirting is an art, an act, an instinct. If you find someone attractive, you get those instinctual butterflies. You feel perkier, sit up a little straighter, and get a little flushed. Flirting is a game that doesn't have to lead to anything. Whether you get to the finish line depends on how you play. You can certainly have fun along the way.

The score never interested me, only the game.
—*Mae West*

One of the biggest flirts I've ever seen is a friend of ours, Amado, a Lebanese man. He's the sort of guy who gets himself bumped up to first class every time. He's irresistible. We chartered a catamaran to sail in the Caribbean, and Amado joined us. He's one of those men who loves women and makes every woman feel special, that she's the one. He fixed on an adorable member of the crew. He was relentless and kept after her the whole cruise. When she got up in the morning, her face would drop if he wasn't at the breakfast table. She would brighten whenever she saw him. The game was on and it was fascinating to watch him hunt.

What's wrong with making people feel good? No harm done. He made her whole trip.

I was charmed one night when I took my seat next to an ambassador at dinner. As he pulled out my chair, he said with a radiant smile, "Where have you been all my life?"

I liked him already. I know the line is clichéd, but his warm greeting set the tone for the evening and made me feel good. There's nothing like an ardent man!

BEING ELEGANTLY PROVOCATIVE

- **The gaze**—Look into his eyes a few beats longer.
- **Mona Lisa smile**—A small, alluring smile can grow to a radiant one.
- **Soft, low, provocative voice**—You will both need to lean toward each other, drawing his attention to your lips.
- **Be affectionate to yourself**—caress your body—rub your arm or your shoulder. It's enticing. He won't be able to take his eyes off your hand and your skin.
- **Reveal different angles.** Throw back your head when you laugh, twist a bit in your chair.
- **Play with your hair** or tuck it behind your ear.
- **Laugh at his jokes**—but don't overdo it.
- **Keep up the banter.** Being light and playful keeps the energy high.
- **Touch his arm lightly**—only the briefest of touches and only above the belt unless you're playing footsy.
- **Be a bit elusive and mysterious.** Don't tell him your life story at a cocktail party.
- **Show him you're interested** without giving him your business card. If he wants your number, he'll ask for it.

I don't think people flirt enough. People are far more flirtatious in Europe, but nudity is more accepted there. A naked body is an object of beauty in a European film. In the United States, nudity is only in R movies. Instead of sex, scores of people are killed off. I just don't get it.

Let's say you've had a good conversation with someone at a party or a chance encounter, and you have to move on. There are ways to give a man a second chance to pursue you. It's an awful feeling to go home, thinking, "Shoot, I should have followed up somehow." If you're at a party or a club, you can always make your way back to the object of your interest and say, "I wanted to say good night. I really enjoyed talking to you." If the feeling is mutual, he will ask for your number or suggest getting together. If you met in a restaurant, a bank, a shop, find an excuse to go right back to connect again by pretending to leave a little something behind.

Where to Find a Good Man

Women are always asking me if I have anyone I could set them up with—the eternal question. Why do they need to be set up? There are men everywhere if you look! Of course, if you don't put yourself out there, you'll never meet anyone. One of the reasons I love the Village and downtown New York is that it's so full of life on the street, with bistros and cafés where people mingle. It's very much like Rome, where you meet people on the sidewalk.

Go to parties or events—you never know who you'll bump into. Go out with men, even if you're not madly in love with them. Who knows? You might like one of his friends. It's always easier to get a man when you're in the company of another man than with a group of women. Go out with a male friend. Both of you will have better luck. It's like a team sport. It's better for you to be with a player of the opposite sex. Men are competitive. If they see you are with a guy, they will want to win you over.

If you don't like to go to parties, try online dating. I have a well-to-do friend from California who went on millionaire.com. She was hesitant but finally thought, "At least I might find a guy who's not after me for my money." She starting corresponding with a man from Australia and found they had a lot in common. They chatted all the time with e-mails, then Skype. They fell in love on the Internet, met, and married. They spend half their time in California and half in Australia. So there's hope! What have you got to lose?

If you want to meet a man, go where men are to be found. Here are some places where you might meet your match:

- Cigar bars—go with an escort.
- Supermarkets—mingle in the produce section.
- Tech shops—damsel in distress
- Gyms—boxing comes to mind.
- Upscale men's stores—discuss ties.
- Tennis clubs—join a threesome to make a foursome.
- Bookstores—pick a section you're interested in.
- Museums—for cultivated types
- Sporting goods stores—fit for life
- Courses—stay away from flower arranging.
- Embassy parties—packed with men
- Art galleries—especially openings
- Long plane trips—business and first class are the best.
- Bed Bath & Beyond—men are usually lost in home goods.

Remember when dropping a hankie was an opening for a man to come to a woman's assistance? That coy move does have a modern equivalent. Let's say you've noticed a man at a café who has obviously noticed you. You've smiled at each other, but he hasn't come to your table. You could always drop something as you walk by to visit the powder room or as you leave. Spilling the entire contents of your purse could be a little overboard. Try something more subtle like a pen, glove, or your headphones.

If you really want to meet men, consider changing your career to urban real estate. A friend of mine recently divorced her husband, who was less than ideal. He was an incorrigible flirt, not terribly responsible, and insisted that she contribute half of the household expenses—and they had four children. In her work as a real estate broker, she met many well-heeled men—many of them looking for a place to live after divorcing. The right man came along and swept her off her feet. She started a new life with a man who appreciated her and her children. Rare—but it happens.

Decorators, too, seem to have their choice of single men. Men are either eager to start over or need help creating a home. I'm not seriously suggesting that you change your profession—I'm just giving you a way of looking at the world as a fishing pond. There are needy men everywhere who would welcome you into their lives. The truth is that a man without a good woman is nowhere. And they know it.

Men are easy to get but hard to keep.
—Mae West

Keep Mae West's words of wisdom in mind. If you haven't found the man for you, don't give up hope. It takes serendipity. It's often when you've given up and stopped worrying that the right man comes along—when you least expect it. You never know when or how a man will show up in your life. You might "meet cute" as they do in the movies, or your first encounter might be more mundane. It doesn't matter how it happens. So start every day open to the possibility that you will be in the right place at the right time and good fortune will smile on you.

THE RIGHT TYPE

Ask yourself these questions before you make too much of an effort:

- Does your heart skip a beat when he walks into a room?
- Does he make you laugh?
- Does he put you on a pedestal?
- Is he truly single?
- Does he listen to you?
- Do you have to fight him for the mirror?
- Does he have or want kids?

How to Make a Man
Feel Good About Himself

Let the man be the boss—or at least let him think he is the boss. Though women really run the world, it's not so hard to give a man the sense that he is calling the shots. Ask questions and let him talk about himself. They love that. Even if you disagree, make him feel important, successful, and smart. Laugh at his jokes no matter how bad you think they are. Compliment him in front of others. When he sees himself reflected positively in your eyes, he'll be proud of himself—and he'll associate that good feeling with you.

> Every man I meet wants to protect me.
> I can't figure out what from.
> —*Mae West*

A man wants to make you happy and to take care of you. Make him feel good by showing him that you appreciate what he does for you. Thank him for planning a date and comment on what great choices he made. Make it clear that you can't wait to see him again.

Maybe his gifts leave a lot to be desired. It doesn't matter what the gift is, it's that he got you one. Love everything he gives you and don't forget to say thanks. Now, a pen or a set of salt and pepper shakers may not be what you had in mind. Even if you're disappointed, try to respond with enthusiasm. (You don't want him to stop giving you gifts, do you?) Gradually you can direct his choices so that his gifts really do thrill you. Toss the L.L.Bean catalogs and replace them with ones from Tiffany or Victoria's Secret.

How to Intrigue a Man

One of the best ways to intrigue a man is not to be too available. Arrive at a party with someone or leave with someone else. You'll seem to have your choice of men and not be on the prowl. But it's perfectly fine to arrive alone if you have the right attitude. This is where your flirting technique comes in handy.

> Don't come crawling to a man for love—
> He likes to get a run for his money.
> —*Mae West*

Don't wear your heart on your sleeve. Playing a little hard to get will only make you more desirable. If you are too easy a conquest, chances are a man will lose interest in you. Don't drop everything when you have a new man in your life. We've all had girlfriends who disappear when they are involved with a man. The fuller your life, the more interesting you will be to a man. So keep your schedule full and don't always be available. Don't turn your whole life upside down to be free in case he wants to go out. You want him to feel you don't need him to be happy. On the other hand:

> Don't keep a man guessing too long—
> He's sure to find an answer somewhere else.
> —*Mae West*

Finding the right balance between being inviting and not being too available is the key to seduction. If he doesn't seem to be running after you, you have to turn him down now and then. Some mystery about how you are spending your time is enticing. But make sure to suggest a future meeting. "I'm so sorry I won't be able to make it that night. I hope we can get together another time" would do the trick. Don't ask him where he's been or with whom. You want to seem secure in yourself.

Men are fascinated if you seem to intuit things about them. Maybe knowing his sign in astrology will give you some insights into his character. Know before you go. Google is a lifesaver. You can find out a lot about a potential new man, but never let him know you've googled him. Be careful how you use the information—you don't want to seem like a stalker. But know before you go. Find out his interests so that you are able to talk about them—politics, sports, gardening, whatever. You don't have to take an intensive course, you just have to be able to ask enough good questions to impress. Wikipedia will do.

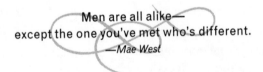

Men are all alike—
except the one you've met who's different.
—Mae West

Men are intrigued by women who are a little controversial and charmingly outspoken. You don't want to overwhelm the poor guy, but being just a little brazen can make you stand out. If you do it in the right spirit, it's lively. The last thing you want to be is boring. In the end, a combination of sex appeal, confidence, and curiosity about the world is what will draw men to you.

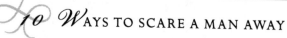

10 WAYS TO SCARE A MAN AWAY

1. **Being aggressive.** Men like to take the lead. There are subtle ways to let them think it's all their idea. There is an old adage: "A boy chases a girl until she catches him."

2. **Being needy and too emotional.** Just the right amount of independence is a good quality. No man wants to get involved with a demanding basket case.

3. **Giving too much information.** There's a lot to be said for an air of mystery. You don't have to reveal your life story immediately. It's better to give him glimpses of yourself over time—let him tease it out of you.

4. **Sending too many gifts, cards, e-mails.** Women tend to be generous and thoughtful, but don't get carried away.

5. **Leaving personal voice mails and calling too often.** Don't drink and dial.

6. **Inviting him to events.** It's fine to ask a man to join you, but keep it to a minimum. Let him ask you.

7. **Saying "I love you" before he does.** Don't assume too much too soon.

8. **Leaving personal belongings behind.** Don't unless you've been invited to.

9. **Asking for a key or offering a key too early.** Way too presumptuous.

10. **Snooping.** However tempting, it's not a good idea. You would want him to respect your privacy.

What is most important is that you let men know that you find them fascinating—nothing works better than admiration.

It's also nice to have a signature scent that he associates with you. The sense of smell is a powerful part of sexual attraction. I know when Alex is away, I like to throw on one of his coats when I walk the dog. I wrap myself in the coat and turn up the collar. I smell him—and it's as if he's with me. Leaving a hint of your perfume on a pillowcase, towel, or bathrobe can remind him in a very sensual way that you are there.

How to Avoid the Walk of Shame

Ah, the walk of shame. You are dating someone and you have stayed over without having planned to. Yes, I was single once upon a time. You have to navigate leaving his apartment the next morning and getting home. It wouldn't look good if you had prepared for a sleepover, particularly for a one-night stand.

Some women consider the morning after to be the walk of "blame." Don't forget, it takes two to tango. Once you make the decision—do I stay or do I go?—don't regret it. If you leave, you are more than likely to have the opportunity again. If you stay, enjoy it.

One way to avoid the walk of shame altogether is to have the man sleep at your house. But that isn't always possible. These things can happen spontaneously—passion is passion, after all.

You could pull a Dracula and slip away before the sun comes up. You could leave a note—maybe lipstick on the bathroom mirror—draw a heart or write *xoxo*. A note should be simple and heartfelt. You could even leave a note that simply says, "Wow!"

Put on your big sunglasses. Hold your head high when you walk by the doorman. You have a choice—befriend him or avoid him. You might need help getting a cab that early in the morning or appreciate his watching you get to your car, so I'd vote for making a new friend.

If you wait until your date wakes up, you should make your exit matter. It's all about that little makeup bag in your purse. You certainly want to look good in bed or near the bed when he opens his eyes. Brush your teeth with your finger, wash off the previous night's makeup, apply a light morning face and a splash of perfume, whether it's his or your own.

If you don't want to look as if you're headed back to the club, you can ask if you could borrow a shirt. Getting into a cab or your own car in evening wear is like wearing a neon sign—embarrassing. Make sure you grab his most cherished shirt or sweater. If you have his shirt, you have a reason to give him a call or for him to call you.

Depending on what's on your calendar that day, you might want to stay for breakfast, but only if he asks. If he doesn't invite you to breakfast, don't take it personally. Be lighthearted and upbeat—stand tall and walk out the door.

How to Break Up with a Man

There is no easy way to say good-bye, especially if he doesn't want you to leave him. It's always difficult.

If you have to hurt someone, you never know what he will do. Of course, it is better to do it in person or in public places so that you can walk away. But if you know the person is going to be destroyed, it's kinder to allow him to receive the news privately so that he can retain his dignity. This is why I find a note works best if he can't handle it. Don't send an e-mail. It is much too impersonal. There is something about a piece of paper that you have touched that has more meaning.

Usually, your decision to break up with someone doesn't happen in a flash. It takes awhile to make the final break. During that period of indecision, you can give him subtle hints to lessen the devastation.

I once dated an Italian soccer player. Before I broke up with him, I prepared him for the inevitable. I sat him down on one of the terraces at Villa d'Este on Lake Como and told him I didn't know where our relationship was going. We didn't seem to want the same things. He knew he wasn't going to be the father of my children, and I intended to have children. And he knew I was considering returning to the States. We both knew that the relationship wasn't going to last. I went off to Marbella with Honey, telling him I needed time to think. Of course, I had already made up my mind, and he knew it.

When you do break up with someone, be brief and vague. Try not to use clichés. Don't go through an entire in-depth analysis of what went wrong with the relationship. There is no point in having a long discussion. You've already decided. Don't be persuaded to try again.

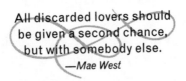

All discarded lovers should
be given a second chance,
but with somebody else.
—*Mae West*

No matter what—it's never his fault. It's better to take the blame. Take the higher ground. Be as calm as you can. Try to steer any conversation away from being an emotional confrontation. Don't allow a scene. Avoid contact with your former boyfriend until he is less emotional and time has healed his wounds. I believe keeping friendships is always better if possible. After all, something about him did appeal to you once.

What to Do If a Man Breaks Up with You

If your relationship fails and you've done everything humanly possible to please him, you have to think that it's his loss and that the relationship was not meant to be. This is where fate and destiny come into play. I'm a big believer that a better man is just around the corner. Be assured that you'll find a man who recognizes how amazing you are.

Sure, it hurts. I know from experience. I had my heart broken by my first love. When I was working as a nurse, I had an adorable boyfriend. I was devoted to him. It turns out he was having an affair with someone else, and I walked in on them. It was a complete surprise, and I was utterly devastated. To this day, I still remember how painful it felt. He tried to get me back, but it was too late.

When I look back at the relationships in my life, I can see now that each was a stepping-stone to a new relationship. The trauma of that breakup pushed me from being a nurse in Connecticut to commuting to New York to model, and catapulted me to living in Europe. Out of a terrible experience and a failed relationship, I changed my life. Sometimes a breakup is a blessing in disguise.

Don't make a scene. Try your hardest to hold back the tears or your delight. And don't get angry. Be as noble as you can. If you cry, it's okay. There is nothing wrong with making him feel guilty!

*H*OW TO GET A MAN TO STAY IN LOVE

The Element of Surprise

One element of seduction that has contributed to the happiness and longevity of our marriage is surprise. Alex will never forget one caper I planned to surprise him. I had stayed behind in Switzerland while he went to Marrakech to race his Aston Martin in the *Rallye du Maroc.* My wise, best friend Zilia inspired me to surprise my husband and reminded me how important an element of the unexpected is in a marriage.

I organized the children and the nanny in Switzerland and invited one of Alex's oldest friends, Richard, to travel with me to Morocco to help me pull this off. At Alex's hotel, I arranged for a big basket of sumptuous fruit to be delivered to his room, along with a note from the hotel manager that a special surprise would be arriving.

Richard and I shopped all day in the souk for the perfect *djilaba* I planned to wear for the surprise. I wore a white and gold veil, and all that was visible were my heavily made-up eyes. I knew I had achieved my goal when the staff of the hotel bowed to me as I walked down the hall on the way to his room. I was unrecognizable. I looked like a Moroccan princess.

I had planned to slip into the room and wait for his return, but I heard voices behind the door. I kicked my heels off into a corner of the hallway and knocked on the door.

He opened it and stood there baffled. I said nothing and salaamed with a flourish into a low bow. He was dumbfounded. Finally, he called to his friend, "Henry, somebody sent us a woman!" He continued to ignore me. "Who do you think did this?"

Carrying myself regally, I walked past him. I bowed once more and sat down without saying a word, giggling behind my veil. I realized he had no idea it was me.

Alex was getting desperate. "Henry, who could have sent her? You didn't send her, did you?" He started moving closer to me.

Of course, Henry knew in advance that I was behind the veil. I'd let him in on the joke. I'm adventurous but not crazy.

I couldn't take it anymore, so I pulled off my veil. Alex stepped back in utter disbelief. He was flabbergasted. He hadn't suspected that I was the mysterious princess. He had no clue. When you expect someone to be elsewhere, it takes a while to believe that person is actually sitting in front of you. It took him three days to get over it. The memory of me dressed like a Moroccan princess still makes him laugh, and he tells the story to everyone to this day.

If you want to breathe new life into a relationship, plan a surprise. Be unpredictable. It's up to you to keep it fresh—and covert operations are fun to plan. Take him to Vegas, a concert, an island getaway. Leave a trail of candy and lacy lingerie up the stairs and to the boudoir for your husband to find when he returns from a business trip.

On Making the Effort

We do so much in our lives that it's easy to lose sight of what's important. Often, our partner is near the bottom of the list. But we women usually put ourselves last. It's so easy to give up on yourself, to skip the gym and to put whatever you can find to eat into your mouth as you race through the day. It might surprise you—taking care of yourself is the key to keeping a long-term relationship alive. You have to take time for yourself in order to be a delight. It's the little extra things you do that will keep your man happy. You need to restore yourself routinely. You have to put yourself first some of the time. It makes a world of difference, and it shows on your face.

> Love is the only industry
> which can't operate on a five-day week.
> —*Mae West*

It's so easy to get caught up with our children that our husbands get pushed aside. You have to make time for your partner and to take care of him. When you were first dating, he was the center of your universe. You would never have been tired and grumpy then. You should make an attitude adjustment and show your partner how much you love him.

Time is the key. If you can get up earlier than the rest of the family, do it. You'll be surprised at how much you can get done in those quiet hours. It's a good time to get organized. There's nothing like starting the day ahead—and you avoid early morning chaos, too. The more you do, the more you get done.

Look Good for Him

I think I have French blood—Canadian, that is. I'm powdered and polished by the time I come to breakfast. Really, I always brush my teeth as soon as I get up and apply a little blush. Remember how much time you used to spend to get ready for a date? Why doesn't the father of your children or your longtime love deserve the same attention?

Look your best—who said love is blind?
—*Mae West*

Your partner is out in the world surrounded by women who care how they look. If you want to keep your man passionate and his eye from wandering, pay attention to how you look.

We've talked about grooming, but your grooming should be kept a mystery. There is no reason for him to know the details. If you are using a mud mask, do it behind closed doors. Same goes for plucking your eyebrows, waxing, or having your roots touched up. Let him think you're naturally beautiful.

Something Special Each Day

Try to do one nice thing a day for your partner—something just for him. It can be as simple as making him his favorite coffee in the morning or bringing him the paper. You can leave him love notes now and then, or call him at the office and tell him you're thinking about being with him after the kids go to bed. Make a dish that he loves or order in from a restaurant he enjoys. Encourage him to work out, because you want him to be healthy and buff. Thoughtful rituals can elevate his self-esteem. Pleasing someone is an effort, but if you have a decent man, you want to keep him and he will appreciate you. Even the simplest of gestures will do. Every day I try to thank Alex for something, no matter how mundane it might be. He loves it.

You really need to consider what makes him happy. It might not involve you. If he seems stressed and doesn't want to talk about it, give him some time alone to unwind. Talking about it might not help if he hasn't processed whatever is bothering him. That's how men are. At the end of a workday or after a business trip, he might need some time alone to regroup. Don't feel offended if he wants to read the paper or watch a game on TV for a bit. Be sensitive to what he wants. Don't criticize him and try to impose your will on him.

> Some women pick men to marry—
> and others pick them to pieces.
> —Mae West

Respect the man you fell in love with. Value him as you did then. Understand that not everything has to be shared in a relationship. You both deserve privacy and a life somewhat independent of each other.

As you do special things for him, he'll start being more considerate of you. Make a fuss whenever he does anything thoughtful or romantic. If he sees that something he's done has made you happy, he'll do it again. Your partner really does want to make you happy. If he comes home to an exhausted, unresponsive woman, he'll give up. It's that simple.

At the end of the day, you want to be able to rest your head on his shoulder and feel that you are protected, and he wants the comfort of home.

On Not Treating Your Partner
Like a Girlfriend

Your partner is not your girlfriend, so don't treat him like one. Let boys be boys. Since I grew up with four older brothers, I was lucky enough to have an inside look at how men really are. My brothers are easygoing, the genial, family-oriented kind. Knowing and living with my brothers made me very comfortable with men, because I understood how simple they are in contrast to women. If you were enchanted by your partner's masculine traits at the start of your relationship, and now he's falling into the girlfriend role, it's a recipe for conflict—or disaster.

It takes very little to make a man happy. Men usually don't care about the nuances. They don't try to second-guess. They are more straightforward than women and far less emotional. And they don't see what we see.

Have you ever asked a man how an event was? The response is usually something like, "Nice." If you asked a woman the same question, you'd get a detailed description of the people there, what they wore, what was served, the flower arrangements, what music was played. It could go on and on.

If a man is upset, and you ask him what's wrong, the typical response is, "Nothing—I'll get over it." A woman would go on for an hour with a blow-by-blow account of what happened, what her reactions have been, how other people perceived it, and how she is thinking about dealing with it.

Most men's idea of torture is having to listen to women chatter away among themselves. Men are so direct that they really can't understand what we talk about and how convoluted our logic can become. Women feel better when they talk about their problems and solve problems by talking them through with a sympathetic listener, considering the problem from all angles. When men hear you have a problem, they naturally want to give you a simple solution, which is not what you're looking for to make yourself feel better. So don't torment your husband by going on about how you are feeling, why you are angry, or how to deal with a problem in great detail. That's what girlfriends and therapists are for.

You need girlfriends in your life to give you emotional support, too. Men really are different, and it should be that way. That's why we have GNOs: girls' nights out. If you go to the movies with your man, skip the chick flicks and don't take him to a restaurant for ladies who lunch. And forget yoga class. There is a reason the class is filled with women; men can't stretch the way women can.

I love men and appreciate our differences. Don't lose sight of the fact that we are fundamentally different and that nature designed us to balance each other. The tension between yin and yang is real—it's what chemistry and attraction are all about.

Making Special Occasions

It is so important to set aside special times and reserve nights for our partner. We do it for our kids all the time, and our partners deserve the same treatment. It's a balancing act. Making special time for each other has to be a conscious decision, because romantic time alone is one of the first things to go as our lives get more complicated. Having a regular date night will make a place for romance in your lives. Alex and I love to go for walks on the beach after dinner under the stars. We meet up in various parts of the world without our children. We have our favorite restaurants wherever we go, and we love dinner and a movie.

It might be as simple as taking a walk during the weekend. Every now and then, a romantic weekend getaway will give a relationship a needed boost. If you offer to watch a friend's kids, I'll bet she'll watch yours. If you can't get away, make it a special weekend—prepare his favorite meal and eat by candlelight after the kids have gone to bed, or see a sexy foreign film.

It's worth investing in some sexy lingerie, particularly for special occasions. In Europe, women wear red lingerie for New Year's. Men love lingerie that's lacy, suggestive, and a little naughty. The key is surprise. Stay away from the nude tones.

Sometimes you might find yourself so busy that you have to plan for sex. The more sex you get, the more you'll want, and it will bring you closer together. Being playful in the privacy of your bedroom will make your husband a happy man.

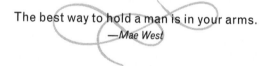

The best way to hold a man is in your arms.
—Mae West

It's important to share things other than your children. You can develop new interests together. You might start collecting art or antiques, learn a language, or play a sport. If your man loves golf, I suggest you take it up. Otherwise you'll be spending at least one day of the weekend on your own. I became a good skier because Alex loves to ski. I finally did go helicopter skiing and learned how to powder ski. I'd keep falling, but I just got back up. It was great to be alone with Alex at the top of the world, skiing the virgin slopes of the Alps.

If your husband is on a business trip, make sure you schedule a private time to talk. Let him know how much you miss him and his warm body. Text-message or e-mail love notes to him. If you start planning special times for you to be together in a relaxed way, your partner will reciprocate.

Guys Will Be Guys

The only place Alex and I really argue is in the car. We both like to be the driver. When I first met him, his hobby was race car driving. What's sexier than a man who loves to race cars? I don't know why driving together is a challenge, but it just is. My parents always argued in the car, and they were married for fifty years.

I guess that's why Alex loves his classic car rallies so much. He goes away with his friends for a week and plays. He won the Tour de France once and has come in third twice. He has a wonderful time, and he can relax because I'm holding down the fort. It's different if we're traveling together—we tend to be concerned about the children at home. I did a rally with him once—the famous *Concorde d'Elegance* held at the Villa d'este on Lake Como, owned by my husband's cousins the Droulers. That event was more a celebration of a car, rather than time and speed. Since north, south, east, and west didn't make a huge difference, there were no conflicts, and we actually enjoyed the ride.

I'm so happy that he can do what he really loves. When he wants to relax, he reads his classic car magazines, and I read the "girly" ones. I don't interfere. It's great if you share his interest, but you don't have to. I can't think of anything more boring than looking at a car magazine. He might like to play golf or to sail. If you're not interested, his time away will give you a chance to pursue something you are passionate about. I like to go to art fairs ʾnd the world with my friend Kim, who is an art adviser. She ces me to her world, and she enjoys showing me how the art world operates. I get to learn, and sometimes I buy. I understand when Alex wants to see his friends without me—just as I enjoy spending time with my girlfriends.

So if your husband likes to watch football on television and you don't, appreciate that "found" time. You can soak in a hot tub, read a book, or take the children to a movie. If he likes to fish, he might want to go away with his friends to fly-fish. He deserves to have interests of his own and a life outside work and family, as do you. If you make it easy for him to follow his interests, he'll be happy to reciprocate when you want to go to a spa with your girlfriends or for a night on the town.

If you have shared passions as a couple and interests on your own, what could be better? It keeps a relationship fresh and gives you something different to talk about.

(PHOTO BY MARILI FORASTIERI)

Seduction Makes the World Go 'Round

$\mathcal{E}$VERYDAY SEDUCTION

Seduction doesn't apply only to love and romance. Grand passions are great, but everyday seductions add something special to life. We all want others to respond well to us and to be happy to see us. We want our daily encounters with everyone from our housekeeper to our doctors, from our contractor to our children's teachers, to work in a satisfying way. The secret to winning people over is to be attentive, caring, considerate, and appreciative. The Golden Rule is part of it. When you think of it, treating others as you want to be treated is a fail-proof technique for good relations with anyone who crosses your path.

The Laws of Attraction

If you behave a certain way with people, getting them on your team is rarely a problem. If your body language and eye contact make you appear open, people will instinctively respond well to you. Being inviting and approachable makes all the difference. The way you speak, the expression on your face, and the way you look at a person encourage a mutual exchange.

Being friendly is such an important quality. I was sitting in a café the other day, and a couple stopped to ask me for directions. They ended up being Italian, and we spoke in their native tongue about Italy and Italian restaurants. We had a terrific conversation. So when people ask for directions, be helpful. (And remember, a man might be asking a question just to get the conversation going, just to have a reason to speak to you.)

The world is a happier place if people are glad to see you and respond to you with real warmth and enthusiasm. You tend to get back what you give out. If you acknowledge the people you encounter and treat them in a way that makes them feel special, they will usually respond to you in kind. If a shop is bustling and a salesperson is harried, your saying, "You must be exhausted after a day like this. I'm impressed by how you manage it so well," might be just what she needs to hear. There is no kindness more basic than to be open and responsive to the feelings of others. In your conversations with people you encounter everywhere, be sensitive to their moods. Empathizing with others will go a long way toward winning them over.

You don't have to be super-smart or the best-looking woman around to charm everyone you meet. Without too much effort, you can be charismatic. Just spread the goodwill around.

$\mathscr{J}$UST THE RIGHT DEGREE OF FRIENDLINESS

When new neighbors move onto our street, I take them a pie to welcome them to the neighborhood. Who does that anymore—especially in New York? When you do things like that, you never know who is going to answer the door. One time, the door was opened by the man of the house, who took me on a tour. He invited me to stay for coffee, but since his wife was nowhere to be seen, I decided against it. You have to know your boundaries.

My father was a contractor who built the homes in the neighborhood in which I grew up. I was always around on the job sites, so I spent a lot of time with carpenters, plumbers, and electricians. It's natural for me to be friendly, as they were such a part of my everyday life as a kid. When dealing with tradesmen, I've learned a fine line has to be walked.

If you go out of your way to be nice, they generally will do more for you. They'll stop by to check on the job or to help. They take your phone calls of desperation when no one else is to be found. Joe, our wonderful contractor for our house in the Hamptons, used to ask my father to play golf. On the other hand, some workers can take advantage. They might think they can get away with a lot because you are nice and don't make relentless demands of them. They'll say, "This is a wonderful project," and then come in way over their initial estimates. Or they take forever to finish. Even worse, some never get around to completing the job.

Finding the right balance between treating tradesmen like professionals who know their job and second-guessing them by being detail-obsessed and micromanaging is the issue. In some circumstances, friendliness has to be balanced with firmness. But it can be done with a smile.

*T*HE KINDNESS OF STRANGERS

People always seem ready to criticize and find fault. It's just as easy to compliment people on a job well done or any part of the job that is praiseworthy. People will be a lot more cooperative if you praise them and throw compliments their way.

You know that compliments work as a conversation starter in social situations, but complimenting people in other situations can also be seductive. Be sensitive to what matters to people and what they are proud of. You might have a teacher's conference and notice that the teacher is wearing that cute holiday pin. Don't hold back. She put herself together that night to look good for the parents of her students—and that means you. The receptionist at your doctor's office might have an outstanding feature—gorgeous auburn hair, a great smile, or brilliant blue eyes. Being complimented on an exceptional quality never gets tired. It makes people feel good.

> Being complimented on an exceptional quality never gets tired.

I often compliment people on their children. You can always find something you like about a child—the baby is adorable, what a good little artist, the school friend is well mannered. Children are their parents' pride and joy—the most direct way to get to a parent's heart is to admire their kids.

Compliments can ease charged relationships. The children of a new boyfriend, for example. They may feel shy or resentful, but a well-chosen compliment can draw them out. "You've gotten so good on that skateboard. Do you watch the competitions on

TV?" or "I'm so impressed that you're reading the last volume of the Harry Potter series. Have you read them all?" You win over a child by making them feel good about themselves, especially if you're a potential stepmother.

$\mathscr{A}$ PLEASURE TO SERVE YOU

Have you ever walked into a shop and found the salespeople unfriendly, or acting as if they're doing you a favor to help you? It happens to me all the time. Do not be intimidated. They forget sometimes that their job is to provide service, not to ignore you.

Select the most approachable, best-put-together salesperson you can find. Ask her, "How are you? Are you having a good day?" Explain that you need help. Ask her opinion, and you might compliment her style. If you establish good rapport with a salesperson, get her card so you can call before shopping next time. I've known salespeople to set aside clothing in a favorite customer's size before a sale.

If you have big department stores where you live, try consulting with the personal shopping service most stores provide. I rely on my personal shopper. She knows the entire stock of the store. Once a shopper knows your style, your preferences, and what's in your closet, she can keep an eye out for you. And the service costs you nothing.

*A*N APPLE FOR THE TEACHER

Noel used to bring apples to school for his teachers. It's an old-fashioned custom. Think of Adam and Eve!

We all want teachers to like our children, to see all their good qualities. And then we go to parent-teacher conferences. They always start out with the good stuff—how great your kids are. As they make their way down to the bottom of the page, they inevitably reach the point at which they make some sort of comment that indicates your child is less than perfect. You know the drill.

I follow their lead. I praise them for all the good things they've said, because that's what we really want to focus on. When it comes to the less-than-perfect things, I express faith in the teacher's ability to fix them. If there are problems, I try to be helpful in arriving at a common ground so that we can solve the problems together. Rather than being defensive, I try to get to the heart of the matter and to show respect for the teacher's judgment and professionalism. You want your children's teacher to find you and your husband gracious and respectful. The goal is for them to know that their opinion matters to you and that you are ready to work with them for the benefit of your child. What is more flattering than that?

If all the kindness and understanding just isn't working and you feel that the teacher isn't the right person for your child, it's time to go to the top. Talking to the head of the school can give you insight into the situation. Remember to praise the teacher's efforts and to stay cool and calm. You don't want to develop a bad rapport. It could affect how your child is perceived. You might ask for a special counselor to help.

My children have so many teachers that I'm relieved that group gifts are organized by the class mothers. That way, a teacher is likely to get a gift that he or she actually wants, rather than dozens of scarves or mountains of fancy soap. If group gifts are not given at your children's school, try to give gifts that are personalized rather than generic. Going to the trouble to know about a teacher's interests or remembering what your children have told you makes your gift special. At the end of the year, I send the children in with a personal gift, usually flowers or sometimes gifts that I've bought at school fund-raising events.

Not the Nanny Diaries

I've had a lot of wonderful nannies over the years, but it took me a while to find Rosie. Some nannies are so spoiled it's like having another child. You have to make a nanny or sitter feel valued— whether it's the level of her pay, the food she eats, or that she's treated like a member of the family—but remember that she's working for you. Don't cater to her every whim. I include Rosie for some meals and share an occasional glass of wine. It's all part of making such a relationship work. What's important is that they understand their position in the household.

It's essential to go over what is expected and to have a routine. Scheduling a weekly meeting can prevent problems from escalating, but can also serve as a time to praise what has gone well. We always observed the nanny's birthday, and the children would make special cards or presents. We gave holidays, sick days, and special days off. Little tokens of appreciation keep nannies and housekeepers happy—pull a flower from an arrangement for her room, and pass on those party bags.

WHAT WOULD I DO WITHOUT ROSIE?

Recently, Bethenny, my *Real Housewives* costar, came over to give Rosie a cooking lesson. She learned how to make carbonara sauce. We opened a bottle of wine, and all enjoyed the meal as Rosie and I shared our advice on men. Rosie knows how to do everything and is great with the kids. If you have household help, you want them to feel as if you couldn't live without them and that they are important to you. If you treat household help kindly, you will get good results. Be aware of your tone of voice when you give instructions. Always sound appreciative. If you want to criticize something she has done, communicate and explain what you want clearly. It's all about communication and respect. You need to develop a good working relationship.

If you want to get your housekeeper to do something she normally doesn't do, show her yourself how it's done. Take the crystals off a chandelier that needs to be cleaned or get up on a ladder to reach cobwebs on the ceiling, and make sure you have insurance. If you are asking for something extraordinary, offer to pay a little extra.

THE DOORMAN KNOWS EVERYTHING

Since we live in a townhouse, Rosie is the doorman in my life (and I'm the concierge). But having a doorman in New York can certainly make life easier, especially for things like receiving packages and calling for taxis. If you don't have one, you can adopt the doorman in a neighboring building for his services. They can always use extra cash. Sometimes you can even arrange to have deliveries made to the other building, and your stealth doorman will hold them for you.

If you're lucky enough to have a doorman, it's a good idea to have daily exchanges with him. Since they know all of your business and that of everyone else in the building, it's best to keep them on your side. If you are a favorite tenant, they'll go that extra mile for you. Maybe they'll buzz up to you when a package arrives—they usually hold them—or put a delivery from the butcher in a fridge in the basement. Always tip them for anything extra that they do. If you do so consistently, they will be quick to help you with your luggage and packages and will hail you a cab on a rainy day. Around the holiday season, it's customary to give them a larger monetary gift for everything they've done for you that year.

Don't forget that a doorman can be a great source of information about the neighborhood—where the best Indian restaurant is, a good shoe repair place, or the most reliable dry-cleaner. He can recommend cleaning people who work part-time for others in the building, good painters, movers, and drivers. When I'm in a neighborhood I don't know well, I rely on the kindness of doormen.

WALKING THE DOG

It might seem decadent to pay someone to walk a dog, but most of us in the city don't have yards for our dogs to play in and our pets need fresh air and exercise several times a day. Thank goodness for our dog walker, Paolo. He also walks Bethenny's dog, fittingly named Cookie. Our dog Aston is nicknamed Monster—so Paolo deals with Cookie-Monster a few times a day.

Having a white dog is an issue, particularly in New York, and I have asked Paolo to go beyond the call of duty to take Aston to the groomer. Also, he often dog sits when we go out of town. I feel it's important for him to know how much Aston means to the family and how much we trust Paolo to take good care of our much-loved dog.

I take the time to make sure Paolo is aware that I view what he does as important and how much I appreciate his doing a great job. Aston loves him. Paolo even taught him to roll over and give his paw.

*G*ATEKEEPERS

Receptionists, secretaries, assistants, and associates are the gate-keepers. There is no better way to the boss. Make it your business to know their names and use them. Chat them up whenever you meet. Single out your favorite and praise her to the boss. Treat assistants with respect—they may be powerful and capable of helping you. Bring treats when you have an appointment—a flower, candy, a coffee. If you see each other often, you might want to give him tickets or invite her to an event. Little gifts or tokens of appreciation could put you on the top of her priority list. If you are good to the staff, your call might just get put through or returned first. They all want to advance, and you want them in your corner. You never know where they'll be a year from now.

$\mathscr{B}$FFS

What would we do without our girlfriends? We can call them in the middle of the night, cry on their shoulders, and share our joys, or our deepest, darkest secrets. In a way, a very good friend is like a therapist, something you should never expect of your husband. Since my husband travels so much, my girlfriends are especially important to me. We keep each other company by having meals together, going to parties, movies, and the theater, shopping, and just hanging out.

When I moved to Europe, I lost touch with many friends, including girlfriends from school days. We change as we get older and so do our interests. What you shared with someone as a child might not seem significant after you move away, marry, and have children. Friends play different roles in different periods of your life. Sometimes you have a blood sister, and you are bound together for life. Other times, things have changed, and you move on.

An old friend from high school, who now lives in Ohio, saw me on *The Real Housewives of New York City*. Tammy contacted me via the show's e-mail. After all those years, we picked up where we had left off. She flew to New York to visit, and we got to reminisce about high school and our pasts. We were so comfortable together—as if we had not been separated by so many years. We still e-mail each other and continue to keep in touch. It's never too late to reconnect.

Having lived abroad and having traveled with and without my husband, I have friends all over the world. I love meeting new people and expanding my social network. Victoria's godmother, Maria, is Spanish and lives in Madrid. Noel's godmother, Anna, is also Spanish and lives in Switzerland. We maintain long-distance relationships with both of them. E-mail certainly makes it easier, but we call often, too. We plan trips to see each other when we can, with or without the kids. We sometimes meet Maria and her husband in the South of France. The last time we were there, they sailed in and invited us to stay a few nights on their boat so we could catch up. We go skiing in Gstaad with Anna and her kids. Anna is a translator at the UN, so she's hard to pin down. We make it a yearly tradition, and we stick to it—otherwise we wouldn't get to see each other with our busy schedules. You have to put an effort into maintaining friendships and that means staying in touch. Even if you don't speak all the time, you know she's there.

Zilia is my soul sister, who is always there for me. Lucky for me, she moved from Monte Carlo and is free to spend time with me in New York. We have a lot in common. She's a Taurus like Alex and me. We share many of the same friends, have the same fashion sense, and both believe in the importance of family. I value her advice in so many areas of my life.

Zilia and I met in Switzerland at a dinner party given by a mutual friend, and she promptly invited me to her house for dinner. She's a model hostess, generous with her heart and her time. She's light and has an energy about her as though she's always ready for a good laugh. She had been in the fashion business, working with the French label Jiki, an evening-wear line, involved in every aspect of production.

Alex calls her Wife #2, because she's always present and willing to help. She's become part of the family. She has helped me to move houses in Switzerland three times and get settled into our new place in New York. She even helps me to edit my closet. It's hard to imagine a better friend. Often lifting my spirit, she's like Honeychile and has become a mentor to me.

When you really need somebody, your acquaintances might run in the other direction. A good friend will be standing by your side.

And, of course, I now have a group of new friends—the "housewives." Sometimes circumstances in life can bring new friendship. Our paths might not have crossed if the show hadn't brought us together. Now they're my new extended family. You can pick your friends, but not your family. So I got lucky.

Maintaining a friendship takes effort, similar to a marriage. In our busy lives, we have to make the time to see each other, support each other, and generally be good to each other.

THE GREEN-EYED MENACE

Honey always told me there is no room for jealousy in our lives. "Get rid of those friends, so you have room for the new ones," she'd say. You all know a jealous woman when you see one. They can't help making snarky comments. They are judgmental, negative, uninspiring. They are the masters of hidden insults that smart. Those masked insults are intended to make them look or feel more important.

Honey and I were invited to a dinner in Marbella by another princess friend of hers, who was hosting a very grand evening replete with notable people—the mayor of Marbella, the Hohenlohe clan, and Sean Connery. Honey's friend was very inviting at first and seemed pleased to see us. She dragged me away from Honey and led me to a table where she introduced me to everyone, including Sean Connery, who was seated to my right, and indicated that I should have a seat. How generous of her, I thought—what an honor to be seated next to Sean Connery. Then she went off, seeing to the other guests.

Just when the first course was about to be served, she came over and said to me, "Oh, no, this is where I'm sitting." She had me leave the table, saying, "You're over there somewhere."

I was so embarrassed. I got up from the table and wandered off to find another seat. There were four or five tables of ten. Honeychile, once again, saved the day. "Oh, come and sit with me, darlin'," she said. It turns out, Honey had never really liked this woman and wasn't surprised that she had made a power play. The princess wanted to show how important she was and to put me down at the same time. Her attitude was obvious. "Who are you to be sitting at this table?"

As for Sean Connery, he looked baffled and disappointed. She was an older women—a tad bitter and unhappy—who took great joy in making everyone aware of how important she was. "Don't feel bad," Honey said wisely. "She would trade places with you in a minute."

*H*OW TO ASK FOR A FAVOR

When you ask a favor, make sure you really need one. Be sure it's someone who is able to deliver on what you request. Be aware of how much you are putting someone out. I once asked a friend if he could help my niece get a job. With the job market being what it is today, I didn't realize how much I was asking. She did get the interview, but not the job. In retrospect, that's all I should have asked for in the first place.

Be careful not to ask too many favors of the same person.

There are limits. If you always show up asking for something, you are likely to exhaust your credit or make someone feel used. You'll know if you've stepped over the line, because they'll stop taking your phone calls. Repay the favor in a thoughtful way—invite them to dinner or to a party, give them a small gift, or do a favor for them in return. You should always send a note of appreciation. Make sure whatever gesture you make is heartfelt.

My girlfriends and I often lend each other accessories and clothing. It's a great way to expand your wardrobe. However, I make a practice of never borrowing anything that I can't replace—whether in value or sentiment. That reminds me of a funny twist on that principle.

Maria, Victoria's godmother, asked if she could borrow a cream Chanel bag for a wedding. She had seen me wear the bag often and had always admired it. I gave it to her gladly. During the reception, the bag somehow got stained. Being a responsible borrower, she took the bag to Chanel to be cleaned—only to learn that it was an imposter. I had had the bag made for me in Italy years earlier, and you really couldn't tell the difference. Maria, who shopped at Chanel and knew the staff well, was mortified, but then she laughed, because she never would have dreamed it was a fake. I guess the lesson here is that you should be careful what you lend to your friends—especially the ones who shop at Chanel.

Only ask your closest friends or those with kids the same age to babysit or help with a birthday party. I drove eight excited boys from Manhattan to the Hamptons through a northeaster for Noel's last party. The activity was paintball and his friends were to sleep over that night. I had to set up for the party. Luckily, my friend Barbara came to my rescue. Much to her shock, I was juggling eight boys, a piñata, cake, and balloons. That's a true friend.

"Can you introduce me to . . ." People are always asking me for an introduction to someone they would like to meet. I have to make certain that the person they want to meet is interested. That is not always the case. If not, I tell them the person is busy, out of town, on crutches—take your pick. So, if you ask to meet someone and it doesn't happen, don't press. You might be able to ask a second time, but a third time is out.

I generally make a phone call and arrange a drink date. Sometimes I even host a dinner party. In most cases, I feel I should be there for the initial meeting to make introductions and ease any sort of awkwardness.

*N*OTES OF APPRECIATION

Nothing feels better than to get a note in which someone is grateful and expresses appreciation for what you've done. It doesn't have to be a major effort—it can be as simple as, "I appreciate everything that you've done for me." In fact, I often sign off with "much appreciated." People like to know that you are aware of their effort—it's more than just a thank-you. When I worked as a nurse, it meant a lot when a family sent a letter or a gift to the unit in appreciation for our work. It made all the difference.

*F*UND-RAISING

This is where friends, connections, and big hearts come in to save the day. If you're asking people for money, I think it's important for them to see where the money is going.

For example, we've invited many friends to Myanmar with us, because we are involved in humanitarian work there. My husband is someone who looks to the future. He has a long-term vision that runs in his blood. He was involved in the Asian markets very early; he visited Myanmar and was fascinated by the country, once the jewel of the British Empire. We bring our friends to Myanmar, a place most have never been, and share with them our love for the country and the people.

We've been doing this for many years and have managed to raise money for fresh drinking water wells for entire villages, costing only one hundred dollars, and for setting up orphanages and schools. My husband films our experiences during the course of our trips, and we show the footage to our friends at home. After a recent monsoon, we reached out to our friends who had visited Myanmar and those who knew how important the region is to us. They sent whatever money they could.

It doesn't have to be a gala—it could just be a phone call. There are so many charities and so much need in the world. Find a charity that's close to your heart and work passionately for it. Your passion is what matters. If you believe in the cause, your commitment will shine through, and people will give generously.

Rather than just writing a check, it's important to give your time as well. If you watch *Real Housewives,* you know that I work with homeless people who want to get their lives back on track through the Soho Partnership. I was so moved to go to their graduation, to see how people's lives had been changed. They were no longer living on the street and were putting their lives back together. I raise money for the American Cancer Society and took the time to visit Hope Lodge. I like to know more about the people on the receiving end.

We had been donating to the Auditory/Oral School of Brooklyn, but Alex had never visited the school. When he did, he was blown away. These kids had been considered retarded, dyslectic, or severely learning disabled. When they were tested and given sophisticated hearing devices to correct their previously unknown hearing problems, their lives turned around. Many of these kids have been mainstreamed. Seeing these kids inspired Alex to show the school to other people who would be as impressed as he was. That's how to raise money! If you've seen the work being done, you can really be persuasive about the importance of your heartfelt mission. Your passion comes through when you are asking people to contribute, and nothing is more convincing.

I send personal notes with invitations to charity events, make phone calls to friends, and bring people together to form a table. It's a good excuse to see your friends and to help a charitable organization at the same time. I invite my friends as guests to join tables I've reserved, and they invite me to their tables in return.

Remember, if people are generous and donate to your charities, you should reciprocate. If you want to raise it, you have to give it. You may not be able to send a check to everyone who asks for a donation, but you may be able to give of your time. You can volunteer to work for the charity or to help raise money yourself. Being there for people can be life-changing—for you and the people who benefit from your charity. Anything you do out of the goodness of your heart is usually rewarded one way or another.

Afterword

Voilà—you know how I like to try new things. I've always wanted to share my stories. The diaries I've kept since 1990 have come in handy. In the end, I feel as if I've written three books—etiquette, advice, from table settings to how to walk in Jimmy Choos, and my own story. I've tried to answer all the questions for those of you who have reached out to me. I am really the person you see on the show. The camera doesn't lie.

If you haven't already learned from watching the *The Real Housewives of New York City*, you'll know after having read my book that a countess is no different from anyone else. My goal was to show you that even if you're not born into the rarefied world of high society or married into it, you can learn manners, sophistication, and grace. Even if you haven't gone to finishing school, "class" is something you can have. It's all about feeling good in your own skin and making other people comfortable. With this skill or ability, you can be dropped anyplace in the world and get along with people from all stations and walks of life. I also wanted to share my perspective on how to incorporate the basics of elegance and style into your daily life.

I set out to give you practical advice on how to travel through the world with ease, but even more important, I hope my insights and stories inspire you to change your life. I wanted to refresh your mind and memory about what it means to have manners, which seem to have gotten lost in the world in which we live today.

I would love to know what you found helpful in my book and what subjects I didn't get to that you'd like to hear about. I'll be blogging on my Web site, www.ClasswiththeCountess.com and www.BravoTV.com, so be sure to look out for my tips. Don't hesitate to send me your questions or comments. I'd love to hear from you. Who knows? I had so much fun writing this book, I just might start another.